C000147374

RECIPES *from* BRIXTON VILLAGE

MISS SOUTH

WITH CONTRIBUTIONS FROM THE TRADERS OF BRIXTON VILLAGE

KITCHEN PRESS

RECIPES FROM
BRIXTON VILLAGE

First published in 2014 by Kitchen Press, 1 Windsor Place, Dundee, DD2 1BG

Text copyright © Miss South, © Brixton Village Grill, © Cornercopia, © Casa Sibilla, © Elephant, © El Rancho De Lalo, © Etta's Seafood Kitchen, © Fish, Wings & Tings, © Jalisco, © Kaosarn, © Lab G, © Okan, © Restaurante Santafereño, © Senzala, © Snugg, © Sponge and Cream © The Agile Rabbit

Illustrations copyright © Kaylene Alder www.kaylenealder.com
Graphic design, typesetting and front cover by Anti Limited www.anti-limited.com

All rights reserved. No part of this publication may be reproduced, stored in a retrieval system, or transmitted in any form or by any means, electronic, mechanical, photocopying or otherwise, without prior permission of the copyright owners.

A CIP catalogue record for this book is available from the British Library.

ISBN: 9780957037342

Printed and bound by Martins the Printers Ltd, Berwick-upon-Tweed.

This book is for all the traders in Brixton, past and present. As well as their recipes, they offered me their time, their expertise and their welcome and made me feel at home here. This book could not have been written without them.

And special thanks to everyone here (and anyone I might have forgotten):

Felicity Ackerley, Kaylene Alder, Sam Allen, Craig Almond, Lambeth Archives and staff, Black Cultural Archives and staff, Ita-Tunde Aworeni, Imran Bashir, Dario Bellantoni, Hari Beaumont, Louise Bolotin, Joseph Bickley, Ed Broughton, Nikki Broughton, Etta Burrell, Paulina Byrne, Joby Catto, Valerie Catto, Donna Corley, Camellia Cosgray, Brian Danclair, Isioma Daniel, Emily Dewhurst, Tim Dickens, Sherri Dymond, Anne Fairbrother, Lindsay Faller, Alicia Green, Victor Greetham, Emy Gray, Giovanni Giovinazzo, Cindy Handson, Gareth Hodges, Bobby Holder, Nicholas Horton, Stuart Horwood, Alex Holland, Zoe Jewell, Ella Killingley, Keith Lewis, Bill Linskey, Hernan and Maria Fayardo and family, Lindsay Marsh, Frankie Murray, Wilson Porras, Hammant Villa Patel, Vanessa Pelz Sharpe, Alan Piper, Motoko Priestman, Iain Riley, Tabitha Rout, Zoe Robertson, Yexali Sanchez, Ida Schaeffer-Allen, Rebecca Schaeffer, Paola Sibilla, Tanapol Srinimtra, Sharmila Subramanian, Binki Taylor, Titi at MTK, Roberto Urban and all the staff of the restaurants and stalls I interrupted when they were working.

CONTENTS

INTRODUCTION

AN INTRODUCTION TO BRIXTON VILLAGE

They say London is a series of interlinked villages, but Brixton is more like a republic. So unlike anywhere else, it never gets referred to as 'London' when it is talked about. It is always 'Brixton' as if it is independent of the other aspects of this vast city. But within Brixton, there is a Village.

Once known as Granville Arcade, this listed 1930s covered market has been reborn as Brixton Village where a group of traders have created a unique mix of shops, cafés, restaurants and stalls that support and reflect the ever-changing community of Brixton.

You won't find the find the delights of Rosie's, Cannon & Cannon, Dombey Meats or Esme's Grocer in this book: they are all in neighbouring Market Row. This book shines a light firmly on the former Granville Arcade, nestled between Pope's Road and Coldharbour Lane. Here is Brixton Village.

Built to the designs of Alfred and Vincent Burr, Granville Arcade was developed and opened by Philip Granville-Grossman in May 1937. The third of the three covered markets in Brixton, it was built to allow market traders to trade up from street stall to permanent premises in order to expand their businesses in an environment less affected by the weather than the barrows on Brixton Station Road or Atlantic Road.

In the early part of the 20th century, Brixton was regarded as the finest shopping area in London outside the West End. The railways provided easy access for out-of-towners. As well as the flourishing markets, department stores such as Morleys and Bon Marché attracted people from far and wide, including a certain Mr Selfridge who briefly owned Bon Marché before opening his own famed business. Both British Home Stores and Marks & Spencer started out in the area, with Marks & Spencer opening in Arch 25 on Atlantic Road in 1903.

For Philip Granville-Grossman, it all added up to the perfect environment for his new project: Granville Arcade, the largest covered market in London. Along with Reliance Arcade, Market Row and the street markets on Electric Avenue and Brixton Station Road, it would form Brixton Market as it is still known today.

Granville Arcade was opened on the site of the former Carlton Club to great fanfare on 6th May 1937, the week before the Coronation of George VI. Popular Danish film star Carl Brisson cut the ribbon and was so mobbed by the excited crowds he had to be carried back to his car for his own safety. The crowds hadn't just come to see him though, and they stayed for the quality stalls and the demonstrations of labour-saving devices by the Ideal Home Exhibition and continued to shop there for many years.

Over time, the traders in Granville Arcade changed and developed as the make-up of the area altered. The market had always featured a wide variety of units and stalls but by the mid-50s it began to specialise in foods and items popular with the burgeoning Afro-Caribbean community. It also allowed recent immigrants from these communities to find work and open businesses in a city that had not always been welcoming. Enterprise and integration happened naturally.

The word spread and people came from all over London to buy fish, fruit and vegetables that often couldn't be found anywhere else in the capital. The market also became a social destination: as well as doing their shopping, people dressed up, caught up on what was happening and kept in touch with each other. Even Edna Marleng, the wife of the Chief Minister of Jamaica, visited while they were in London in 1956.

Stalls were owned by the same families for years, and the staff and their customers formed real relationships over time. People had certain traders they preferred and were loyal to them. It was very much a retail market and service was as important as quality of items: very few of the stalls were self-service. Some of the floor to ceiling shelves that harked back to this era of shopping were still visible until the refurbishment in 1996.

By the 1990s, Granville Arcade's popularity was waning. Well-known stalls such as the Bible bookshop, the bakeries, the pet shop with the famously foul-mouthed parrot, the clothing boutiques and the record shops had begun to close and the building was feeling its age. The newer South American community in Brixton moved in but this failed to stem the decline.

In 2006, the Granville Arcade was sold to new landlords, London and Associated Properties (LAP), who hoped to bring it back to its heyday as 'London's Largest Emporium'. The controversial decision to change the market's name to 'Brixton Village' (without any consultation with traders or community) had been taken in 2001, but didn't really stick until LAP took over. It was hoped a new name would lead to new fortunes.

Those new fortunes were not quite what the shoppers and traders expected. In January 2009, LAP unveiled plans to redevelop Brixton Village and build a ten storey, 111 apartment block above it. Current traders would not be given preference and there was no guarantee that the market would retain any community aspect.

The idea shocked Brixton. A consortium of traders and Brixtonites – including the head of the Brixton Market Traders' Federation Stuart Horwood, councillor Alex Holland and local resident Paul Bakalite – came together to oppose the project. They planned to get the Village listed by English Heritage on architectural grounds and so halt the development but the arcade wasn't deemed to be architecturally important enough and the bid failed. Undeterred, the consortium re-grouped and contacted the Black Cultural Archives and sought to have Brixton's three covered arcades (Brixton Village, Reliance Arcade and Market Row) listed for their cultural significance to the local Afro-Caribbean community.

In April 2010, after many months of work and campaigning, they were successful. English Heritage declared that the value to the community of covered arcades in Brixton Market lay "in its past and its current traders and shoppers and the meaning the market has for them". It was the very first listing in the UK to take the positive impact of post-war multiculturalism into consideration, and the buildings were given Grade II listing. They now cannot be altered or changed in a way that does not preserve this aspect.

Saved from radical redevelopment, the Village still lacked the energy and dynamism of the past and over 20 units were empty. In May 2010, LAP sold it to new landlords InShops, who specialised in market spaces. In turn, they approached community organisers Spacemakers Agency to come up with a radical scheme to attract new traders to the market. It worked: 98 applications for the spaces were received in one week, and by Autumn 2010 the empty units were filled with a mixture of pop-up shops, artist spaces, community shops and new restaurants.

Food had always been something that linked the various communities in Brixton and it quickly became something that galvanised Brixton Village. More restaurants opened, along with new boutiques, and the weekends began to be busier again for the whole market. As the word of mouth about the market's revival grew, the traders lobbied the landlords to increase the opening hours into the evenings too. Suddenly Brixton Village was the trendiest place in London. People who had always seen Brixton's differences as an issue now saw them as appealing. From *Time Out* to *The Observer* to *The New York Times*, the resurgence of Brixton Village was everywhere. Queues for some restaurants were extensive. The traders' hard work had come to fruition.

Some traders were able to move on because of the demand for the units: the French-African grocers, the Filipino café and the roti shop all changed hands and use. But some people felt left behind as Brixton Village seemed to gentrify, and others worried that too many traders lacked enough of a connection with Brixton or the Village's retail past. That debate continues. Brixton Village has been sold yet again to new landlords Groupe Geraud, and for some there is a feeling that the market and landlords still have work to do to welcome local residents who live in the surrounding area, one of the poorest in England. However, it cannot be denied that the improved fortunes for Brixton Village have been beneficial for many in the area, especially the traders in the market who run stalls and supply the new restaurants.

Brixton Village would probably be more recognisable to Philip Granville-Grossman today than any other time in the last 40 years as its fortunes rise and, as he intended, it brings people to Brixton to shop and eat and relax under the vaulted ceilings and natural light of the beautiful building. The sounds may have changed from Dexter Dix, the house pianist at Wheatlands piano showroom in 1937, through the soca, calypso and reggae music of the last 40 years to the sounds of cutlery on plates, but Brixton Village still has a lot to say to the people who use it.

A CHANGING MARKET

by Anne Fairbrother

Anne Fairbrother of Cornercopia was one of the original traders to start operating in the rejuvenated Brixton Village. Cornercopia remains a strong and lively presence in the market today.

Nowadays Brixton Village has quite a reputation for food. **Time Out London** named Brixton Village the best place to eat in 2011 and the market regularly makes appearances on 'Top 10' lists around the world. Its eateries pop up in publications like the Eurostar **Metropolitan** magazine, **ELLE Japan** and **Condé Nast Traveller.** Yet less than four years ago it was a very different story.

In 2009 Granville Arcade was partially dead. On 2nd Avenue there were 20 or more empty units falling into neglect. Trade elsewhere was down hugely. But how had it got this way? Supermarket culture, recession, the closure of the car park on nearby Pope's Road: there were multiple reasons, yet Brixton Village was not alone in the UK suffering from empty shop syndrome. Decline becomes cumulative, almost viral. Once a few places in close proximity shut down, people stop going there. The city loses a limb or, in this case, half a market.

Following the defeat of plans to redevelop Brixton Village into flats and its subsequent listed status, things changed remarkably and the speed of transformation has been incredible. The regeneration of Brixton Village in just three years would probably have taken a decade or more elsewhere. Some would argue there has been too much change, but whatever your viewpoint there is a remarkable story to be told. It's a story which wasn't initially about great burgers or cocktails but about people, ideas, creative energy and genuine community collaboration.

What would you do with an empty shop?

News of empty shops up for grabs spread quickly across the Brixton grapevine. Thanks to a partnership between civic ideas agency Spacemakers and Lambeth Council, the units would be rent free to people with good ideas. On a freezing November night in 2009 around 350 curious Brixtonites came along to a 'space exploration' night in Brixton Village. It was the start of the recession and there were many people out of work or short of cash – but not short on energy, ideas or confidence. There was palpable excitement in the air amongst Brixton's artists, activists, makers and doers as Spacemakers and the Council shared their vision for bringing a new burst of life to a market in decline.

We were invited to explore the empty units and to radically re-think their potential, not just as retail units. Signs on the outside of each unit listed their facilities and dimensions. Some units had several electrical sockets and water, but many didn't. The unit that is now Cornercopia's dining room hadn't been rented out in 15 years, and it was lacking water, electricity and love.

Even with optimism and imagination it would have been hard to conceive that two years on this space would be our welcoming dining room, hosting a variety of occasions and meals. Few would have thought then that things would change enough for you to sip a cocktail in the spring light while looking out onto a scene of Japanese tourists mingling with Herne Hill mums, trendy young things Instagramming their lunch and traditional market traders working at their stalls.

What excited us the most on that cold November night wasn't just talking about new shops, but seeing what an empty shop could become: from the world's smallest cinema to a DIY photo booth, a cabaret or a venue for fishmongers and butchers. The brief was wide open to the imagination, but our deadline to submit a proposal was one week. Plans for temporary ideas or pop-ups were welcomed alongside those testing out new long-term businesses. People were encouraged to think about the social nature of markets and the wider role they play in the community no matter what their project was.

What happened next?

A week later Spacemakers had received over 90 proposals from which they selected 30 eclectic ideas. Around half were long-term business ideas, but there were also plans for community shops, theatres and artists' pop-ups that would exist for a few days to several months. Due to the lack of electricity, water and other facilities, it was hardly surprising that in the first wave of new shops, there were few proposals for food outlets.

Except for us. Our proposal was about food – we wanted to test out an idea for a corner shop with a difference – one that sold foods made or grown locally in South London. A place that demonstrated the cornucopia or abundance of foods that are made or grown on our doorstep. A shop that acted as a local hub for food and a place where everything on the shelves had a story to tell, and might spark a debate about where our food comes from.

We wanted to support local market traders by buying their ingredients and encouraging others to do the same. We would provide an outlet for the growing number of local makers and growers to sell produce, from half a dozen jars of tomato chutney to a glut of rhubarb that we could turn into jam. We envisioned Cornercopia as a shop where people could try out an idea for a new food business or make some extra cash. We had ambitions from the very start to run community workshops, cooking classes, market tours and to serve locally sourced food, but we started small.

We had been allocated Unit 65, a corner unit toward the back of the market, with four electrical sockets and not much else. At the time, it wasn't a place where you could cook, so we kept with the idea of jams, preserves and chutneys: things that kept well and could be made off-premises with ingredients bought on our doorstep in the market.

With Christmas just round the corner it was the perfect time to sell hampers of Brixton-made goodies. The first thing we made was our Brixton Market chutney – a plantain and tamarind chutney to take advantage of the plentiful cheap, ripe plantains all around the market. It became so popular you can find our recipe in this book. In just two weeks, with the help of friends, we renovated our shop, filling its shelves with handmade preserves, marinades, pickles and pork rillettes, successfully launching on 17th December 2009.

Most of the other empty units had also been transformed into art galleries, vintage shops, tiny theatres and even a 'shop' to recycle your Christmas trees in January for re-planting in a local school garden. But post Christmas the reality of running a shop six days a week in a freezing cold market with virtually no footfall caught up with all of us.

Days went by with few customers. We made a small amount of money circle the market several times: we sold cups of tea or bowls of soup we had made at home to the other market traders, and then used the money to buy a coffee from Federation or a snack elsewhere. It was a real micro-market economy and group survival tactic which brought us close together. What we desperately needed though was more footfall.

From small acorns...

In the middle of the freezing cold January we organised our first event. We invited food bloggers and well-known supper club hosts to transform some of the remaining empty units for a day. They brought with them hundreds of enthusiastic followers, many coming to Brixton for the first time, and showed us events were the way forward.

Spacemakers and the new traders curated a rolling festival of events and pop-ups to support these fledgling businesses. We hoped to shift focus from the market as a trading space towards it becoming a social space as well. We wanted it to be a place where you might come to meet friends, to be entertained, to learn something new or to trade skills and ideas. A place where curious and unexpected things happened. And we found that thousands of people wanted to join us.

Over the following weeks there were dance performances down the avenues, improvisation workshops amid the vegetables and tiny gigs in the vintage clothes store. Customers were serenaded as they bought red bream, gospel choirs led people around the market like pied pipers and experimental theatre groups brought pyrotechnics to our doorstep. Volunteers organised everything from children's storytelling workshops to tech-days, and hundreds of musicians came to perform for free. We ran market tours and make-your-own events. There was something pretty special happening in Brixton Village.

Once people started coming and staying here in large numbers, they got hungry and provided a great opportunity for food businesses to establish themselves. At Cornercopia we started by selling soup and simple stews and gradually, plate-by-plate, chair-by-chair, we built ourselves a tiny restaurant. Others started equally small, and as some of the pop-ups ended and units became available again, more and more great little food outlets began to appear. The market became more and more edible.

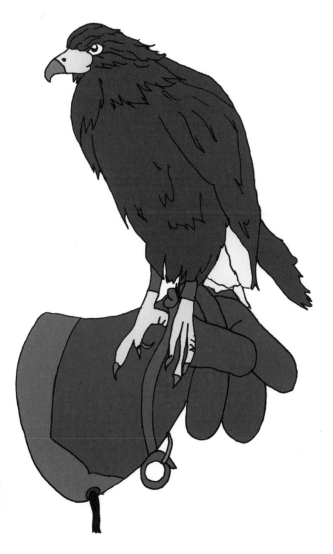

Jay Rayner, local resident and food writer, certainly helped build momentum by telling *Guardian* readers in 2011 that Brixton Village was the "most exciting, radical venture on the British restaurant scene" and recommending the food and the ethos – not least because in a restaurant world where money talks these were independent ventures based on enthusiasm, great foodie ideas and not much more than a trip to Ikea.

New restaurateurs used the existing stalls, enhancing the feeling of community within the Village. They worked together to extend the opening hours from Monday to Saturday days to late nights and Sundays as well. Their businesses complement one another and they remain passionate about supporting Brixton Village as a whole, not just visiting to eat, but to shop, observe and learn from each other as well.

NOTES ON WRITING AND USING RECIPES FROM BRIXTON VILLAGE

Brixton Village has become somewhere very special in the past few years and it seemed the right time to write a book capturing that essence, whether you shop and eat there all the time, have only heard about it or want to know more before you visit.

I hope that the book helps you get a full sense of the market, from the building itself to the traders and customers to the food and produce it sells. With any luck, you will feel like you know Brixton Village as well as I do by the time you've finished reading and cooking your favourite recipes from it. I've been shopping in the Village for the last five years or so and I've watched it change in many ways. However, the friendly welcome you receive shopping or eating there always remains the same.

Creating this book has been a journey in itself. It developed out of a desire to preserve this period of history in Brixton and immortalise the traders' recipes. Every trader selling food and drink in Brixton Village, whether as a restaurant or retailer, was invited to submit recipes for the book – for a variety of reasons, some opted not to. The recipes here fall into two categories: traders' contributions and my own recipes that have been inspired by the incredible produce available at the market. They are a truly global selection of recipes.

The traders have been extraordinary in their response to the project, welcoming me with generosity and enthusiasm and sharing recipes, skills and knowledge. Many have become friends over the writing of the book and I now have to leave twice as long to do my shopping so I can catch up with everyone in the process. Maybe when they see their names in print, I'll get cheeky and ask to skip to the front of the queues on a Friday night too!

I'm aware that not everyone has such a fantastic market on their doorstep and, if you're shopping elsewhere, I've offered substitute ingredients where possible. A list of nationwide stockists will be available on the Kitchen Press website (see the link below). If you are able to come to Brixton, I've given tips on where to start buying things in the area, but don't forget to look around and find your favourite shops and traders as you go. Shopping here really enhances eating out in Brixton Village.

The book may also contain ingredients that aren't familiar to everyone, so we have included a glossary section. Any information that is crucial while cooking the recipe is in the recipe introduction to save trying to turn pages with hands otherwise occupied.

All the recipes in the book were tested before being published here. If, however, you do come across anything that doesn't work for you, please let Kitchen Press know for any future editions.

I am sad to have come to the end of writing this book. It's been a dream first book for me and I've rarely eaten as well as over the months I was recipe testing. But I'm delighted that my favourite part of writing it – learning about Brixton and its people and taking part in the community – will continue for many years to come.

I hope this book will encourage others to do the same and see the real Brixton beyond the *Time Out* reviews. It should also remind everyone that markets are an increasingly valuable community resource that should be used anywhere they exist. I just happen to think there are few finer markets in the UK than Brixton Village...

Miss South

www.kitchenpress.co.uk/brixton

A NOTE ON QUANTITIES AND MEASUREMENTS

Oven temperatures are in centigrade – if you're cooking in a fan oven, lower the temperatures by 20°C. If you're using gas, use the conversion chart below.

All spoon measurements are standard sizes and level unless stated otherwise.

All eggs are large unless stated otherwise.

All butter is salted unless stated otherwise.

All dairy products are whole-fat unless stated otherwise.

All salt and pepper is to taste unless specified.

Gas Mark Conversion Chart

Centigrade	Gas Mark
140	1
150	2
170	3
180	4
190	5
200	6
220	7
230	8
240	9

TRADERS

THE TRADERS

It's worth bearing in mind that Brixton Village is a fully functioning market and the traders and restaurants change all the time.

The list of traders here is a snapshot of the market between February and August 2013. By the time of publication, you may find that the make-up of the market has altered – and this fluidity is part of what makes it so special.

A & N Fresh Fruit & Veg

There are two branches of this store. The first is the greengrocers' stall you see as you come into Brixton Village at the Atlantic Road entrance, sweeping round the corner onto 1st Avenue. It sells a dizzying selection of unusual and tropical fruit and vegetables throughout the seasons. This is where you can get your june plums for juices or caraili for hot sauces or teas. There are alluring hands of sweet little finger bananas and a vast choice of all kinds of mangoes. Mixing self- and staff-service you get the best of both worlds selecting your own or having help if your hands are full.

The second branch is directly opposite Ilias' Fish on 1st Avenue. This yellow fronted store offers much more than just fresh fruit. This is the place to come for wedges of pumpkin cut to your specification, bulging bunches of beetroot with the leaves still on and the teeniest, tiniest velvety soft pods of okra. Step inside and you'll also find Jamaican groceries and essentials like bags of **bammy** or cans of condensed, evaporated or fortified milks for drinking or cooking. You can get your five litre bottles of white vinegar for cleaning meat and fish and sacks of rice of all sizes. Service is friendly and the staff will cut items to size, explain the goods and help you find things on the shelves, all with a smile and a joke.

Recently renovated and given a whole new shop front, the A & N is definitely there to stay, selling a big selection of ripe and ready-to-eat fruit and greeting new or regular customers with equal friendliness.

The Agile Rabbit

The only pizza place in Brixton Village, The Agile Rabbit is the perfect place to linger in the evening while sharing a pizza or to come in the day time for a quick snack. It's equally popular with people on dates or parents with kids after school (albeit at very different times of the day!).

Pizzas are super thin bases with just the right amount of bubbled and blistered crust then dressed with top quality ingredients that make them very moreish. I'm not sure I've ever managed to stop at just one slice...

Owned by Victor Greetham, The Agile Rabbit doesn't just offer delicious food. There's good coffee and great music too. The coffee is any time, but the music is a Thursday and Friday special. There's everything from solo singer-songwriters and jazz artists to bands getting their first break, all helping to bring the music back to Brixton Village.

The Agile Rabbit is always popular and particularly packed with locals and regulars who come for the laid-back atmosphere, the only calzone in town and the neighbourhood feel. The fact you see the same friendly staff shows they feel at home here too. Since opening in 2010, The Agile Rabbit has become as much a fixture in the Village as Victor's hats.

Bellantoni's

Dario Bellantoni has an extensive background in restaurants, having worked in the kitchens of Bruno Loubet, Marco Pierre White and Gordon Ramsay. But it was his local connections to Brixton that made him see the potential in Brixton Village, and he opened in 2010 when few other restaurants had moved in.

From the beginning, Bellantoni's specialised in pasta and soon the lasagne alone was attracting people to the market. They came for thoughtful dishes, quality ingredients and the beautifully cooked fish (you can tell Dario's grandfather was a fishmonger). Dario and his business partner Roberto Urban welcome children, always keeping sweets for them, but it is also the sort of place big kids who have recently left home bring their parents. Nothing says 'I'm doing well' to your mum and dad better than some custom-made ravioli that you can still afford to pay for yourself...

Bellantoni's stopped trading just before we went to press with this book, but Dario and Roberto both have plans for new individual businesses in the area so keep a look out.

Brixton Village Grill

The borough of Lambeth has a sizeable Portuguese population so it is fitting that Brixton Village has its own Portuguese restaurant in the form of Brixton Village Grill. Run by Cidalia Rodrigues and Michael Lythgoe, it combines traditional Portuguese cuisine with influences from former colony Mozambique and is one of the Village's most popular spots.

Unsurprisingly the restaurant centres round its grill, which sears flavour into dishes such as fresh fish (supplied from fellow traders Ilias' Fish), pork ribs, lamb chops and the famed piri-piri chicken. Everything is prepared in their tiny bustling kitchen and the simple but excellent home-cooked food has attracted a loyal following since it opened in April 2011.

Michael and Cidalia have never had their own restaurant before, but Cid has years of experience in feeding family and friends, enjoying nothing more than a table full of happy, hungry people in her house or garden. That friendly feel is apparent at Brixton Village Grill where customers often chat to neighbouring tables in between courses. They come time and again for the fantastic hand-cut chips, the velvety soft chicken liver pâté and the Dime Bar cheesecake that is so legendary people will order it at the start of a Friday night meal to make sure it hasn't sold out by the time they are ready for dessert.

Carniceria Los Andes

If you love pork, then you will love a trip to Carniceria Los Andes or, as everyone calls it, the Colombian Butchers. One of only two butchers in Brixton Village, they offer such a good selection of pork you expect that they might be able to order in the oink as well if you asked nicely enough.

Sheets of pork skin can be used to make heavenly scratchings, while the huge hands of pork (actually the front legs) make pulled pork that will impress any foodie in town. There are also trays of pigs' tails and ears, either salted or plain, which add flavour to beans or callaloo. People come from far and wide though for their chorizo Colombiano: huge plump link sausages, they are bursting with fresh herbs and have whole cloves of garlic in with the chunky pork and seasoning. Fried up and served on a *bandeja paisa*, these sausages are unlike any you've had before.

But if pork isn't your thing, the beef is pretty spectacular too. There's the picanha steak just crying out to be taken home and grilled to perfection (see the recipe on page 46). If you like things wobblier, there's spotlessly clean tripe, just right for a soup or a stew. At excellent prices, everything is cut and prepared to your specifications and you might even get the chance to improve your Spanish...

Casa Sibilla

Casa Sibilla is a true family restaurant and deli, set up by owner and chef Paola Sibilla in 2010. Inspired by her mother's cooking as a child, Paola went to culinary school and realised that she could cook in ways that her mother couldn't. She refined her techniques and embarked on a culinary journey that would take her through Italy and Paris to London.

Having been based in Brick Lane and Marylebone, Paola felt a connection with Brixton immediately, feeling that 'this is my house' when she first came to the Village. It seemed the perfect place to introduce people to proper, regional Italian food rather than what people have come to think of as Italian food.

Though she was born in Turin in northern Italy, Paola's wider family come from the southern region of Puglia and Paola grew up eating two very different styles of food. Piedmontese cuisine is heavier and more dairy-based, while Puglian food is about sun and sea with tomatoes and seafood a speciality. The constantly evolving menu at Casa Sibilla marries together these traditions.

It is not a place to rush and just fill the belly. It is a place to have the best ingredients and to really enjoy food alongside friends and family. Casa Sibilla feels like a discovery: ingredients are sourced from the market and used confidently, wines come from areas in Italy not well known in the UK and the atmosphere is full of possibility. In many ways it feels like you are in Paola's home, surrounded by her family of cooks, making memories as you eat. Paola's recipes will fit into your kitchen easily with simple, delicious dishes to try. You'll see why she says there should always be great satisfaction in cooking.

Brixton cornercopia

Cornercopia

One of the original restaurants that came to the market as part of the Spacemakers' initiative, Cornercopia has grown to be one of its great successes. It has developed with the Village and helped to develop it as well.

Connecting to the community is crucial for owners Anne Fairbrother and Iain Riley. From the early inception of Cornercopia when they only opened for lunch on certain weekdays, they have been involved in projects that centre them in the wider community. Not only is all the food sold in the shop and the restaurant locally and sustainably sourced, they have always worked with Transition Town and the Brixton Pound to make sure Cornercopia has the right kind of local footprint.

This promotes a connection to the produce and the origins of things instead of a detachment from food and creativity. Iain sources everything he can for the restaurant from Brixton Market to allow the ripples from the Village to touch the rest of the area as well.

Iain and Anne brought their units back to life from 15 years of semi-dereliction and have created an environment that was well worth the risk. They now have the shop, kitchen and, of course, the dining room with its wood-fired stove for winter. This expansion has allowed them to help other people take risks through pop-up events such as The Botanical Cocktail Bar in summer 2013.

The food and cooking are as strong as the ethics and Cornercopia has become a cornerstone in the market, always looking for ways to shine a light on those they work with and the Village itself.

elephant.

Elephant

Elephant may be smaller than its majestic namesake, but for many people it is just as impressive. The only Pakistani restaurant in Brixton, its speciality is the kind of intricately spiced food you would eat in a traditional Pakistani home. More meat-based than Indian food, Elephant fills its tiny space with big flavours. Most of the dishes are the childhood favourites of owner Imran Bashir and are heavily influenced by his mother's cooking. Less formal than the 'curry house' style people are used to in the UK, Elephant serves a small menu that people come back for time and time again.

One of the dishes that catches the eye is the *keema*, or spiced lamb mince with peas. Described by Imran as Friday night food, it's a big draw to the restaurant: just the thing to start the weekend with, people queue up for it. They also come for the legendary buttery daal. Imran is the lentil whisperer. I have friends who come to Brixton for this rather than my company, scooping it up greedily before anyone asks to share and then talking about it for weeks afterwards. Marina O'Loughlin, restaurant critic for *The Guardian*, feels the same way about the light crisp samosas.

It's hard to believe Imran doesn't have a background in cooking, but he was in fact a solicitor. The legal profession's loss is Brixton Village's gain. Elephant manages to feel like home even if you didn't grow up in a Pakistani house.

El Rancho de Lalo

Tucked away on 1st Avenue, the white frontage of El Rancho de Lalo is a real landmark in Brixton Village. Always busy and bustling, it's like going inside a Spanish-Colombian home to eat. Proprietors Carlos Zuluaga and Andres Quintero and their families are found behind the counter producing enormous plates of Colombian food in a welcoming environment.

Always popular with Brixton's growing South American community, El Rancho de Lalo provides familiar tastes, sounds and newspapers for those who have moved here. Mixed in with the Spanish speakers are other Brixton locals who have a big appetite and know that El Rancho de Lalo is an excellent place to satisfy it.

The food is simple but packed with flavour like good home cooking should be. Crunchy *empanadas* and blistered corn pancakes (*arepas*) start your meal off, but you'll need to leave room for platters of seared steak, garlicky chorizo Colombiano sausage, fried pork belly and whole tilapia accompanied by sweet plantain, creamy avocado and silky soft red beans. Everything is good, but the soups are sublime. The rich flavourful chicken broth filled with gizzards could cure anything that ails you while the beef soup is fantastically fortifying any day of the year. Every dish here is enhanced by the legendary homemade salsa. Bursting with fresh coriander, spring onions and chillies, it has a tang of vinegar and a warming heat that becomes fearsomely addictive with each mouthful.

Don't come to El Rancho de Lalo expecting small portions of light dishes. The cuisine is rich and hearty with portions to match, but the food is so good you will rarely see anything other than clean plates.

Etta's Seafood Kitchen

One of my favourite spots in Brixton Village is Etta's Seafood Kitchen. Behind the cheery hand-painted purple frontage, it is just like sitting in someone's homely kitchen while they cook for you. A family affair featuring the eponymous Etta Burrell, her cousin Carole and her daughter Cheryl, you can bring your own wine and beer and watch the food being prepared as you chat. Often the seafood is so fresh you see it coming in from the stalls in the market when they are busy.

Etta's was one of the first places to open when Brixton Village got its new lease of life. Etta had always cooked, mainly for film crews as well as family and friends, but had never thought to open a restaurant until she came to the market on an impulse. The market manager asked her for a business plan and Etta just knew she would be cooking in Brixton.

Etta started with just ten pounds' worth of seafood bought from the fishmongers in the Village. Each day the business became more established as she cooked for guests from around the world and friends helped build the kitchen. She is proud to continue the heritage of a market once famed for its fish by being the only seafood restaurant in the area. Etta's recipes remind you that seafood in both Brixton and London hasn't always been beyond people's means and has a history and heritage.

She feels blessed to be able to feed people, seeing food as a joy rather than a fuel. Her simple, well-spiced dishes show off the quality of her fish and seafood and her confidence in her recipes. Everyone is welcomed by Etta's enthusiasm and infectious laugh and encouraged to eat, drink and enjoy each other's company.

Faiz Food Store

The largest grocer in Brixton Village, the Faiz Food Store is quite Tardis-like. Looking like a simple fruit and vegetable stall from the outside, you step past piles of fresh herbs and spinach, in through a narrow doorway and are greeted with food and produce from all round the world.

Specialising in Colombian and South American goods, the Faiz is the perfect place to come for packets of pre-mixed *aliños*, liquid smoke to infuse your food with that barbecued flavour when you can't cook outside, bags of frozen yuca or a vast selection of hominy and dried corn. You can stock up on a wide variety of Caribbean goods such as specialist pulses, syrups and cordials, soft drinks, sweets and crisps. It's a little like being a kid in a candy store. But there are also piles of fruit, vegetables and herbs here at great prices and, if you buy your scotch bonnets here, they often throw a few extra in at no cost.

Until recently, the Faiz was two separate units opposite each other on 1st Avenue, but over summer 2013 they amalgamated into the one store to make the most of what they offer. I doubt you'll leave without making at least one purchase...

Federation Coffee

When Nick Coates and George Wallace left their jobs in the City, they wanted to bring real Kiwi coffee culture to Brixton, so they opened Federation in a small unit on 2nd Avenue in the Village in 2010. An early success story, they have since moved to a larger corner unit on the end of 5th Avenue and there are still queues out of the door on a Saturday morning. They also have a small hatch at the Piano House in central Brixton, making them the only Brixton Village business to have another branch in the area.

Using Monmouth beans from Borough Market and grinding them in Bermondsey and Battersea, Federation have been perfecting their own roast since they opened. Loyal customers say they serve the best coffee in Brixton, and they hold their own on London-wide lists too. People come from 8 a.m. to start the day with Federation's perfectly poured flat whites and their bacon and corn fritters, and to pick up a bag of beans to use at home.

Tables fill quickly, and one can people-watch over the home-baked goodies that are the other attraction here. Offering Antipodean favourites like almond-infused friands and Anzac biscuits, everything is made fresh daily – along with the relaxed atmosphere, it's no wonder Federation has become a centre point of the market.

French & Grace

Created by Rosie French and Ellie Grace, this small but perfectly formed restaurant grew from their popular supper club and award-winning blog, Salad Club. The girls specialise in Middle Eastern and modern British food and are hugely inspired by the produce of Brixton Market.

Wraps are bursting with vivid pink beetroot and perfect creamy white labneh. Plates of puy lentils are like dark green jewels and the mezze plates are glorious with squash and pumpkin. Most of the food is vegetarian but spicy lamb merguez sausages and paprika-infused chorizo sneak in for a hit of flavour.

Everything is freshly cooked and clearly exceptional quality, coming directly from the stalls in Brixton Village and the wider market. French & Grace are also fabulous ambassadors for Brixton, running a stall throughout London and at festivals around the UK as part of the Kerb street food collective. There is always a queue for their food no matter where they sell it and they have no shortage of fans. However, the true celebrity at French & Grace is the soft fluffy flatbread that they are famed for. The recipe is a trade secret, but well worth a visit.

Fruit + Veg

This stall, run by the ever-present Phil, is especially noticeable for its hand-painted sign and the extensive selection of yams and cassava which are all lined up, just waiting for you to try them all. Roots, tubers and starchy vegetables of all kinds are specialities here, from those yams to breadfruit and parsnips.

Tucked in between the Brixton Party Shop and Ilias' Fish, Phil supplies many of the restaurants in the Village and from his excellent vantage point seems to know everyone and everything in Brixton Village. I often nip here to stock up on starches and carbs while waiting for my fish to be cleaned and prepared at Ilias'. I can quite often do both from the same queue and who doesn't like multi-tasking when shopping? It's all part of the service when you shop at independent stores...

FISH, WINGS & TINGS

Fish, Wings & Tings

Fish, Wings & Tings is as much about the culture of cooking as the food itself – it is impossible not to relax into eating here. Owner Brian Danclair has been drawn to feeding people since childhood fish cookouts by the sea in Trinidad. By 19, he had moved to Washington DC and was managing a classic French restaurant. He graduated onto cooking in the south of France in his twenties before coming to the UK for love.

When Brian came to London he was surprised how 'back a yard' or homely the Caribbean restaurants were. He opened his first place above the Dogstar pub on Coldharbour Lane in 2005, wanting to cook Caribbean food with French flair. He made the move to Brixton Village in May 2012 and brought authentic Creole food to the market, mixing Jamaican, Bajan, Grenadian and Guyanese influences with Trini food. There's a little Portuguese in there and a dash of South American – his famous hot sauces are named after his Venezuelan grandmother.

No matter where you are from, there is something for you at Fish, Wings & Tings. Specials from around the Caribbean change weekly and people can't get enough of the codfish fritters and the pumpkin stew with *rotis*. It won't take long to realise it isn't just the kitchen that is open here, but the welcome too. Come for the food, but stay for Brian's hospitality and exceptional selection of rums.

Honest Burgers

Probably the best known outside Brixton of all the restaurants in Brixton Village, this independent burger chain began life here on 1st Avenue. It has recently expanded into new sites in Soho, Camden and Notting Hill and looks set to sweep London with its famous rosemary salt chips and 30 day aged beef from the Ginger Pig Butchers.

Opened in 2011 by Dorian Waite, Tom Barton and Phil Eeles, Honest Burgers specialise in burgers and nothing else. You can choose from beef, chicken or veggie, and they all come with a portion of the rosemary salt chips on the side – once you've tasted either, you'll understand why there is such a big queue for Honest Burgers no matter what time of the day or night. They've teamed up with WAGFree Bakery to include a gluten-free option for the buns, and details like this have helped them keep their loyal clientele as more high-end burger joints have opened around London.

Their food is almost impossible to recreate at home and it's best to visit for the experience instead. Each branch offers the same standard, but Brixton's has the best atmosphere as you can sit outside in the market and watch the world go by.

Ilias' Fish (formerly Dagon's)

In its heyday, Granville Arcade was all about the fish. Fishmongers were scattered throughout the market, each specialising in different types of fish or seafood and each with their own loyal clientele. Only two fishmongers remain today and, until recently, one of them had been owned by the Hodges family since 1953.

Known as Dagon's, it remained a big draw to the Village even when other shops lay empty. As Brixton Village became progressively busier, the queue at Dagon's was still the longest in the building and they also began supplying the new restaurants in the Village. But 60 years is a long time to keep the early hours that Billingsgate demands and in May 2013 the Hodges family sold the business on to Mr Rusi, who owns Jeffries Fishmongers in neighbouring Market Row.

Any worries about quality were allayed as the new Portuguese owners know their fish like the back of their hand. Although the well-known figure of Gareth Hodges with his flat cap and market banter is no longer serving there, other familiar faces such as Donna Corley – the longest serving female trader in the Village – remain.

The queues, especially on a Saturday, also remain and everyone has adapted to the new sign and the new name of Ilias' Fish. It was shopping here that introduced me to the market in general and where I learnt pretty much everything about the area from the staff and the customers. I'm not sure you can say you know Brixton Village unless you've shopped here.

Iya-Ibadan

Named for Ibadan city in south-west Nigeria, this small store on 5th Avenue isn't quite as large as its namesake (the third largest metropolitan area in Nigeria). But it's almost as interesting.

Particularly good for specialist spices such as alligator pepper and *ehuru*, you can also pick up a selection of dried chilli peppers and bitterleaf here. The service is more European than in some of the other stores and you should be able to ask questions about what you are buying whether you are a total newbie to Nigerian cuisine or an old hand wanting to compare regional variations across the most populated country in Africa.

Whether you're coming for the groceries or the social occasion of shopping, you'll be amazed just how much Iya-Ibadan can offer you from such a small store. Bring a big bag to make the most of it!

Jalisco

Run by Wilson Porras and Yexeli Sanchez, Jalisco serves Mexican food to the hungry masses of Brixton Village. Wilson is Venezuelan, but loves Mexican cuisine and is determined to introduce more dishes alongside the tacos and burritos. He knows Brixton Village well, having lived in the area for 14 years, and used to eat at La Cabana Colombian restaurant on the site where Jalisco is now.

People want good food they can enjoy a drink with and don't have to wait too long for, and Wilson and Yexeli provide it. You'll always see the same staff there when you visit and they pop in on their days off to say hi. Regular customers come for the margaritas and I imagine there will be a stampede when Wilson starts to serve Clamato cocktails and micheladas as well in the next few months.

New dishes will be cropping up on the menu too, but old favourites will remain: Jalisco will stay true to the Latin American heritage of the unit.

Kaosarn

Regularly acclaimed as serving the best Thai food in London, Kaosarn was the first restaurant in Brixton Village to find fame: partly because of a glowing review in *The Observer* from food writer Jay Rayner, but mainly because they offer more interesting Thai dishes than most people are used to in the UK. As word of their crisp-skinned grilled chicken, fresh salads and *larb gai* grew, so did the queues outside the restaurant.

Run by Tanapol Srinimitra and his family, the restaurant is just as famous for its service as its food. If you are lucky, the impeccably attired and glamorous Gisele will be seating and greeting in one of her little black dresses. She, her sisters and the rest of the staff know how to keep the queue moving and the plates coming from the tiny kitchen. Because Kaosarn is never not busy, people are happy to sit outside all year round just to get a table here, but the chilli kick in the food warms them up nicely again. Situated on the corner of the Coldharbour Lane entrance, it's a good site for people-watching too.

Loyal customers travel from all over London to eat at Kaosarn, and there was much pleasure among those in deeper, darker south west London when the family opened a second branch in Clapham Junction in early 2013, spreading the Brixton magic a little further afield.

Kumasi Market

The only Ghanaian shop in Brixton, this bright-pink-fronted store sells a wide variety of African fruit and vegetables outside including many types of aubergines. There is also a vast selection of dried fish. Inside you can stock up on groundnut paste for the *nkatenkwan* recipe on page 58. Cassava and banana leaves are delivered weekly and you can also grab Ghanaian CDs and soaps while you are here. Owner Neo will reserve things for you if you ask very nicely!

Lab G

Open since April 2011, *Laboratorio Artigianale del Buon Gelato*, or Lab G, has become a real draw to Brixton Village. Owned and run by chef Giovanni Giovinazzo, it sells some of the best ice cream in the country and attracts adults and children alike. In the summer, people queue outside the market entrance for the famed salted caramel gelato.

Lab G is a little piece of Italy in Brixton. Giovanni serves Italian coffees and liqueurs upstairs in the small hidden bar, but the star of the show is the gelato. The recipes are specially created for the Lab by Giovanni whose aim is to introduce proper Italian-style gelato to the UK. Softer and less sweet than most mass-produced ice cream, he uses a variety of base styles to create his wide range of flavours. Some like vanilla and coffee are classics, but others like *torrentini* (chocolate hazelnut) or *zuppa inglese* (trifle) are less well known.

Giovanni's love of ice cream comes across in the attention to detail in his recipes. Each one is very easy to follow and the possibilities for flavours are only limited by your imagination. Most of the recipes work just as well without a machine, but you'll be tempted to splash out on one when you realise making your own ice cream is so much better and cheaper than buying from a supermarket.

Giovanni's recipes are alchemy and you'll see just why he's created a lab for his talents here in Brixton.

Love Cake Patty

Tucked into the corner of the Coldharbour Lane entrance on 1st Avenue, Love Cake Patty is one of the best-named businesses in the market. There are piping hot Jamaican patties and homemade cakes, and it's obvious how much owners Dennis and Kerensa love to feed the people of Brixton Village. Everything is freshly made on the premises and a well-filled patty costs just £1.20, providing a great lunch on the go or – if the crumbs on blazers are anything to go by – after school snack. Slices of cakes and tray bakes are equally affordable.

Patties are a Jamaican favourite. Not the same as the Cornish pasty, they have a crumbly short pastry, often coloured with annatto or turmeric to give the well-known yellow colour (though, originally, this would have come from using goat fat as the shortening). They are traditionally filled with minced beef, but Love Cake Patty offer a wide selection, from saltfish to spiced lamb to a completely vegetarian *callaloo* version. All have hints of spice and scotch bonnet peppers wrapped in that soft yellow pastry – these are a world away from the pre-packed versions of patties you might have tried before. Be prepared to queue: Love Cake Patty gets a lot of love itself...

L & J Fishmongers

This fishmongers (confusingly called Otto's on the sign) has been owned by the Murray family for over 50 years. A large stall near the Pope's Road entrance, it used to be one of three owned by the Murrays in Granville Arcade's heyday as a fish market. There is little rivalry with the other fishmongers – in fact the Hodges family, who used to own Dagon's before selling up, are cousins of the Murrays. People shop at both stalls, coming as much for the family traditions, interactions and service as the fish. There is a steady stream of customers and on Saturdays the queue can get up to the corner of 3rd Avenue. No corners are cut on quality or service and Jonathan and Frankie will always take time to answer questions.

Their range of fish is impressive, keeping more unusual items such as catfish and live crabs. You can also order your fish, pay for it and come back to collect it if you don't fancy doing the rest of your shopping or going for lunch with a live crustacean or a giant jackfish about your person. There is no excuse not try something new here.

Mama Lan

Formerly a fishmongers, this corner unit on the Atlantic Road entrance has become a landmark within Brixton Village thanks to its beautiful carved wooden front door and its fabulous Beijing dumplings.

Opened in September 2011, the restaurant grew out of a supper club run by owner Ning and her mother. It specialises in the street food of Beijing, in particular dumplings. Not to be confused with dim sum dumplings, these are made from a thicker wheat flour wrapper and are bigger in size. Each one is hand made in the restaurant and you can watch them take shape while you wait for your food. This is a true family business: Ning's mother and aunts ran a stall in Beijing around the time of the Cultural Revolution and, once they moved to the UK, they were keen to show British people that there is much more to the cuisine of the most populous nation on earth than we knew.

The constantly evolving and seasonal menu includes big bowls of noodle soup, spicy chicken wings, pickled vegetables and many wonderful ways with tofu. The dumplings are stuffed with ingredients like wood ear mushroom and beef and spring onion before being pan fried to give a slightly crispy base. They take a lifetime to perfect and are a closely guarded secret, so come at lunchtime when the queues are shorter and try all three varieties on the menu.

MTK AFRICAN RESTAURANT
WE ALSO CATER FOR PARTIES

MTK Restaurant

Tucked away on 6th Avenue, MTK might not have the same profile as some of the restaurants in the Village, but few are quite as continually busy as this simple kitchen. This is even more impressive when you realise owner Titi runs the place almost completely single handedly, cooking everything from scratch.

Open since 2006 and specialising in Nigerian food alongside other West African dishes, MTK serves breakfast, lunch and dinner to a constant stream of visitors, hungry both for the excellent food and the social interaction. The jollof rice on page 52 is a classic Nigerian dish everyone loves, but you must also try the fish. It is all supplied fresh from Ilias', just a few metres away, and cooked expertly. The steamed black tilapia is Titi's favourite dish to cook and the love and skill shines through.

Other best sellers include generous bowls of *egusi* soup, thickened with bitter melon seeds; *moi moi*, a kind of steamed bean pâté; and plates of spicy gizzards that make your whole face tingle with heat. Cool down again with a portion of dodo (fried plantain). You'll see why people travel from outside London to eat here.

If you haven't tried Nigerian food before, you will get the best introduction possible by calling into MTK. It's almost like being welcomed into Titi's home for dinner, but without having to offer to do the washing up.

Okan

Owner Motoko Priestman is originally from the southern Japanese city of Osaka, where people rarely eat sushi. Moving to Dulwich, she began cooking for a living in a jazz club in Camberwell Church Street before touring festivals and street markets. She found a niche around Spitalfields and Brick Lane specialising in fried rice cakes (*yaki onigiri*) and *okonomiyaki*.

She had built up a loyal following by the time she came to Brixton to eat at fellow Brick Lane trader Paola Sibilla's new restaurant Casa Sibilla, and fell instantly in love with Brixton Village. Okan opened in June 2011 and is one of the most memorable units in the market with its beautiful paper lanterns and koi carp hanging from the ceiling. It often has queues outside, especially for the *okonomiyaki*.

Best described as a savoury pancake made with cabbage and batter, *okonomiyaki* is a delicious and healthy meal, usually topped with pork belly. In Osaka they eat it with rice as they have a more carb-based diet than the rest of Japan. Motoko has adapted it for British palates (and vegetarians), adding specials and tofu versions. Even though the name means 'as you like', she hasn't added the non-authentic chicken version people ask for.

Motoko is keen to show people that Japanese food is often very simple and easy to cook, especially now that most ingredients are easier to find in supermarkets. Some of the recipes she contributed to the book are personal favourites that don't feature on the menu in Okan but which are great to cook at home.

Oracle's Organic Juice Bar

Brixton Village's only dedicated juice bar, Oracle also offers vegan and raw foods along with a selection of specialist organic items and provisions. Run by Ita-Tunde Aworeni, Oracle is about eating as healing rather than just fuel.

Growing up in rural Jamaica, Ita-Tunde learned about the importance of plants and food from his grandmother. Connected to cooking and preparing food from a young age, he grew up with the idea of spiritual nourishment being more important than simply sating an appetite. There are no artificial ingredients, including refined sugars, in Oracle's food and drink. Ita-Tunde believes that 'what is sweet to the mouth is bitter to the belly' and offers many other ways to fuel the body than the Western obsessions with sugar and caffeine. His best seller is the spirulina energy juice with avocado, banana and spirulina to beat the 4 p.m. slump. It is particularly good with the vegan raw cake made with dates and raw chocolate.

Food and drink is respected at Oracle. The juices aren't thinned with water and their thick texture needs jumbo straws to do them justice. Preparation isn't rushed and the shop has a relaxed atmosphere that welcomes everyone, from the gym bunnies in need of rehydration to the Rastafarians seeking I-tal sustenance. Luckily Oracle is open six days a week to help them all out.

PJ Horwoods Butchers

Tucked away opposite The Agile Rabbit on 1st Avenue by the Pope's Road door, this deceptively small butcher's counter sells a fantastic selection of more unusual cuts of meat. Primarily catering for an Afro-Caribbean clientele, this is the place to come for your cow foot or cuts of mutton.

Happy to talk you through the best ways to prepare certain cuts of meat, the staff at Horwoods are like the Brixton version of the jolly butchers from children's books. The meat is excellent quality and, if you're unsure what to go for, you'll often get tips and encouragement from the other customers who know their meat almost as well as those on the other side of the counter. They remember regular customers, some of whom have been shopping there for years, and how they like their meat.

Bring a big shopping bag and stock up on black pepper and jalapeño sausages and beef short ribs while you wait for a pizza on a Saturday lunchtime. There is always something worth trying for Sunday lunch.

RESTAURANTE SANTAFEREÑO

Restaurante Santafereño

One of two Colombian restaurants in Brixton Village, Restaurante Santafereño is particularly famed for its breakfasts. People come here, especially at the weekends, for both the food and the social atmosphere that owners Hernan and Maria have created.

A family-run restaurant, Santafereño has been in Brixton Village for seven years, replacing the greasy spoon café that was there before. It serves a primarily South American clientele but is also popular with French-speaking Africans and those keen to be introduced to Colombian cuisine. Santafereño feeds them their famed *caldo de costilla*, or rib soup, as well as hard-to-find flavours of Colombia such as the kiwi-like *lulo* juice or Pony Malta malted drink. They nourish both body and soul.

Everything is freshly cooked and superb value for money. Many meals include a juice such as *guanabana* or a sugar-cane soda. Vegetarians love Santafereño with its vast plates of soft creamy beans and portions of onion tart. However, it is especially good for meat and fish eaters with whole fried tilapia and pork tamales often available. No matter what you order, make sure you bring a big appetite.

Senzala

This Brixton Village favourite sells crêpes and galettes and suits adults and children alike. The buckwheat galettes are gluten-free and there is an extensive vegetarian and vegan selection. It's no wonder Senzala are so busy all day.

Senzala started life as the Brick Box restaurant, partly run in conjunction with the Brick Box collective who programmed music, art and entertainment in the Village in the early days of regeneration. Brick Box have since moved on to other market projects in Tooting and beyond and, in February 2013, the name of the restaurant was formally changed to Senzala. The owner, Claudia Rodrigues de Oliviera, chefs and staff remained the same and so did the regular customers, many of whom come every Sunday morning with their kids.

The menu is constantly evolving to offer people more of what they enjoy. There have been new toppings and tweaks to old favourites. There is ice cream for the kids and the new Brixton Brewery beers for the grown-ups. Art exhibitions line the walls inside and the atmosphere is always friendly and welcoming. Senzala is a genuine neighbourhood restaurant that offers something for everyone.

Sierra Leone Groceries

As the name suggests, this small store on 3rd Avenue specialises in produce and products from Sierra Leone. The fresh produce outside varies from day to day while inside there is a dazzling selection of items. It is best to ask the staff to help you due to the packed shelves and lack of elbow room. It gives a relaxed old-fashioned feel, enhanced by the vast selection of blue and white enamelware outside the shop. Sierra Leone Groceries has the biggest choice of this in the market and it's hard not to pick up a few pieces each time you pass.

It's also worth calling in for bags of skinned black-eyed beans for making batches of *akara* or *oleleh* without having to stand and do it yourself. Don't forget to buy a bigger bag than you think you need – both are so delicious you'll make them time and time again.

Snugg

With its gorgeous glossy red frontage, Snugg is the new kid on the block in Brixton Village. New owner Binki Taylor took the unit over from the Relay tea rooms and has given it a fresh style with sharing platters and evening opening, cocktails and live music, but she's cleverly kept on Relay's chefs Ella Killingley and Joseph Bickley to ensure the incredible quality of the food.

When you hear that Ella has worked for both Ottolenghi and Honey & Co, you won't be surprised that all the food is made from scratch on the premises. Her menu features eclectic modern cuisine known here as 'London food' – a mix of classic English, Mediterranean and African inspired dishes, from the early morning Trader's Breakfast of baked eggs and chorizo, to cake platters in the afternoon and small dishes and cocktails in the evening (or a bit of all of these whenever you fancy it).

Alongside the fresh and original food, Snugg's mission is to bring dancing back to the market. Binki has teamed up with Handson from United 80 to make Brixton Village that little bit louder and get everyone moving. On their opening night, the most enthusiastic dancers were the local kids who were making it a proper block party.

Snugg welcomes you in to eat, drink, chat and dance. Ella and the team make it feel like you've ended up in the kitchen of very stylish friends who can really cook.

Sponge and Cream

Paulina Byrne has been baking since 2007 and first set up Sponge and Cream as a stall outside the former Brixton Village sweet shop in 2011. She had previously spent several years refining her talents at the Hummingbird Bakery in London and creating her own unique style. Each cake she bakes has its own carefully matched flour, all the flavourings come from real fruit and vegetables and she has no relationship with margarine.

Her favourite might be the banana cake, but it depends what day you ask as she loves them all. Cakes are her passion. She has loved baking since she was a teenager and, when she left IT in search of a job she wouldn't complain about, it was the natural option to start making cakes.

Baking cakes for a living isn't quite as effortless as it might look. Paulina is so busy with commissions as well as the unit in the market that she is constantly mixing, baking and icing, but it is obvious she adores her job. She is as welcoming as her display of cakes and people can't resist calling in to finish off their dinner or pick up a treat for themselves or loved ones. She is inspired by American baking, preferring the light crumb of their sponge to the traditional English Victoria sponge. Her red velvet cake is her most popular and now comes in a gluten-free version. She sells the only German chocolate cake in London made with semi-sweet chocolate and when mangoes are in season she buys the best in the market to make her mango cake. These mangoes also make their way into her weekend-only cheesecakes.

Forks at the ready...

Viva Afro-Caribbean Food Store

The largest of the four remaining African grocery stores in Brixton Village, Viva Afro sells just about every African foodstuff you can imagine along with the utensils you need to prepare it. Beautiful bowls sit beside huge carved wooden pestle and mortars and spoons big enough to stir pots for 40 people. A wide selection of dried herbs, peppers and stockfish fill the newspaper-lined baskets outside.

Inside there are shelves upon shelves of appealing tins, bottles and foil-backed packages holding dried prawns, *egusi* seeds and mixes for *suya*. There are containers of palm oil large enough to be classed as a barrel and a huge selection of pastes and spices. The shop is constantly busy with shoppers stocking up on rare cooking ingredients or tastes that remind them of home. In the summer months you often see huge baskets of African land snails outside.

Whether you cook African or Caribbean food daily or infrequently, you will find everything you could possibly need at Viva Afro. And you'll probably discover something new and interesting along the way too.

WAGFree Bakery

Nothing to do with avoiding footballers' wives, this is in fact the Wheat- And Gluten-Free Bakery and it specialises in baked goods for those with coeliac disease and wheat and gluten intolerances.

They offer all kinds of sweet and savoury treats usually off the menu for those who must avoid wheat and gluten. From tiny tartlets to pies, cakes and breads of all kinds, the products are nothing like the heavy lumps of gluten-free goods seen at the hands of less skilled bakers. So good are WAGFree's products, they are sold in other Brixton restaurants such as Honest Burgers as well as in Selfridges and other discerning outlets, and people come from all over London to sample the treats at the tables outside and to stock up for home.

They also stock a range of flours and ingredients for you to try making your own goodies with. One of the few stores in London to keep *teff* for making Ethiopian or Eritrean *injera*, they encourage you to try new things and versions of old favourites. While you're there, try the gluten-free Czech lager Celia, either to drink or to make delicious beer batter for proper fish and chips.

*WAGfree have now moved their production out of the market, and in the unit have teamed up with Martin Vozar to create Vozars, a gluten-free cafe, deli and restaurant. You can still buy their delicious baked goods here, as well as treating yourself to Martin's exceptional gluten-free cooking.

N
S

POPE'S ROAD

THIRD AVE

FOURTH AVE

FIFTH AVE

SIXTH AVE

SECOND AVENUE

FIRST AVENUE

ATLANTIC ROAD

COLDHARBOUR LANE

BRIXTON VILLAGE

MEAT

COW FOOT SOUP

Fish, Wings & Tings

This is a simple but hearty soup. Served at lunch in the Caribbean when people tend to eat their main meal of the day, it will set you up for anything. You'll need a large pot and some time to let it all cook. Ask your butcher to chop the cow foot for you to make it even easier. Don't be squeamish about this cut of meat: it has a fantastic flavour and makes the most beautiful rich beefy stock.

2 large cow feet, cut into 16 pieces

2½ litres cold water

200g yellow split peas, soaked overnight in water

10 sprigs fresh thyme

1 bunch chadon beni (culantro)

1 bay leaf

10 cloves garlic, chopped

1 onion, chopped

1 large stalk celery, cut in 2.5cm pieces

1 red pepper, chopped

1 scotch bonnet, left whole

1 large cassava, cut into 6 to 8 pieces

5 eddoes or coco, quartered

200g calabaza pumpkin, cut in 2.5cm pieces

2 cobs fresh corn, quartered (optional)

salt and black pepper to taste

Wash the cow feet thoroughly and then put them in a large pot with the water and the yellow split peas. Bring to the boil and then simmer for about an hour.

Add the herbs, garlic, onion, celery and red pepper to the water. Keeping it whole so you get the fruity flavour instead of the heat, add the scotch bonnet too and cook for another 1½ hours or until the meat is tender. Check on it during this time and add more water if it looks like it is getting dry. The cow foot creates its own stock so you won't dilute it. If you want even more depth of flavour add a salted pig tail or some beef flank too. When the meat is tender, add the chopped cassava, eddoes and pumpkin and simmer for another 30–40 minutes until the vegetables are soft.

Season and serve the soup in big bowls, as it is. It is a meal in itself and needs no embellishment. Thick and hearty, it brings this inexpensive cut of meat to life.

Brixton stockists note: you can buy cow feet at PJ Horwoods near the Pope's Road entrance. They sell the cleanest ones around and will cut them to any size you need. Cassava is easy to get from any greengrocer. *Chadon beni* is available in the Wing Tai Oriental Supermarket on Electric Avenue.

CARBONARA WITH BRESAOLA

Casa Sibilla

Carbonara is one of those dishes that is so incredibly simple you think it should be more complicated. People debate endlessly over its authenticity, but it's more enjoyable to make it than debate it. While carbonara is commonly associated with bacon or pancetta, this version uses bresaola (air dried beef).

Linguine or tagliatelle hold the sauce better than spaghetti here and is easier to eat.

450g linguine or tagliatelle

6 large free range eggs

200ml single cream

200g Parmesan, freshly grated

200g thick piece of bresaola, cubed

1½ tablespoons water from the pasta pot (if needed)

sea salt and black pepper

Bring a large pot of salted water to a boil. Cook the pasta until al dente. This should take about 10 minutes.

In a large bowl lightly beat the eggs and cream and add the Parmesan and a pinch of salt and pepper. Whisk well until creamy. If it looks too thick, add a tablespoon of boiling water from the pasta pot to loosen it.

Drain the pasta and return it to the pot. Stir in half the egg mixture and half the bresaola and toss it all to combine. Allow to stand for 2 to 3 minutes so the pasta absorbs some of the sauce and toss again. Adjust the seasoning according to taste and divide among serving bowls.

Spoon the extra egg sauce over the top, then sprinkle with the remaining bresaola and serve immediately.

Buon Appetito!

Brixton stockists note: you can buy the bresaola in the deli at Casa Sibilla along with many other beautiful Italian delicacies.

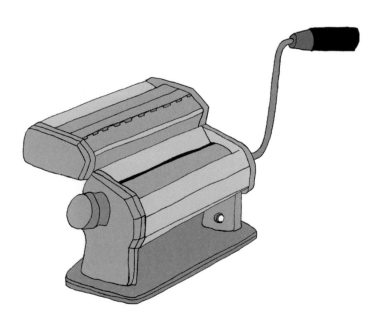

POLPETTI (MEATBALLS)

Casa Sibilla

Who doesn't love meatballs? I certainly do and these are some of the best I've ever had. Light and very tasty due to the combination of two meats, they don't fall apart like some meatballs do, especially if the meat is chilled when you mix it.

2 slices white bread, crusts removed

100ml milk

2 tablespoons olive oil

2 small onions, chopped

300g minced beef or veal

300g minced pork

1 free range egg

50g Parmesan, grated

2 tablespoons flat leaf parsley, finely chopped

100g plain flour

3 tablespoons sunflower oil

sea salt and black pepper

Soak the bread in the milk in a bowl for a few minutes. When all the milk is absorbed, mash the soggy bread into a paste.

In a frying pan, sauté the onions with the olive oil over a gentle heat until softened. Leave to cool down.

Squeeze out any excess moisture from the bread and place it into a large bowl together with the minced beef and pork, the softened onions, the egg, Parmesan, parsley and salt and black pepper to taste. Mix well to combine everything.

Moisten your hands and shape the mixture into small balls about the size of a walnut. Roll them in flour and chill for at least 30 minutes in the fridge.

Heat the oil in a frying pan and then shallow fry the meatballs for about 7 minutes on each side, trying not to move them about too much. You may need to do two batches to prevent crowding the pan or they won't brown properly.

After about 20 minutes, once they have turned brown all over, put the meatballs on a plate to drain and sprinkle with sea salt before serving.

Or if you prefer, once you have sealed them by frying lightly on each side, use a slotted spoon to transfer the meatballs into a pot of simmering tomato sauce for about one hour.

Buon Appetito!

PICANHA STEAK WITH WHISKEY SAUCE

Restaurante Santafereño   Serves 4–6

....

This cut of beef is also known, rather less poetically, as the rump cap. It is a tender cut from the rear of the animal with a lovely cap of fat to provide flavour and keep the meat succulent as it cooks. Bought in a large pieces rather than pre-cut steaks, it is spiral cut which means the fibres run diagonally through the meat, allowing it to stay tender when charcoal grilled.

The whiskey in the sauce enhances the smoky flavours if you are able to cook the meat on the barbecue, and will give a hint of them if the weather keeps you indoors and cooking on the stove. I use an Irish whiskey like Bushmills because we Northern Irish have the oldest whiskey distillery in the world and, thus, the finest in my mind. You could use your tipple of choice.

1kg picanha steak, sliced into 4–6 steaks by the butcher

1 tablespoon sea salt

75ml beef stock

50g unsalted butter

100g chestnut mushrooms, sliced

2 teaspoons Dijon mustard

100ml whiskey

200ml double cream

1 teaspoon black peppercorns, crushed

You'll have to buy the picanha in one piece, so ask the butcher to cut it into four or six steaks as needed. Keep them thick for the best finish. Absorb as much moisture from them as you can using kitchen towels and bring them to room temperature before you start cooking. The steaks are best grilled.

Salt the meat with about a tablespoon of sea salt. Traditionally, it is not seasoned with black pepper – just enough salt to help crisp the fat and bring out of the flavour of the meat to perfect effect. Heat a griddle pan or grill well or get your barbecue ready for use. Once the coals are white you are ready to cook.

Lay the meat fat side down and cook for 5 minutes each side for rare, 7 minutes each side for medium and 9 minutes for well done – plus an extra minute on its side to crisp any fat you have missed. Juices should be rising to the surface of the meat. Take the steaks off the heat and allow to rest for at least 15 minutes – the spiral cut of the meat makes it seem too tough to cut if you don't leave it to rest. You want the juices to keep coming out and the salt to mingle with them.

While the meat is resting, deglaze the griddle pan with the beef stock to lift all the caramelised bits from cooking. Set aside. Melt the butter in a pan and sauté the mushrooms until they soften. Stir in the mustard, then the whiskey and cook out for a minute while the whiskey bubbles: this will remove any raw alcohol flavour and mellow it down. Add the double cream and the beef stock you deglazed the pan with earlier. Stir in the black peppercorns. Simmer the sauce for 1–2 minutes over a low heat.

Slice each rested steak into four thick pieces and serve with the whiskey sauce. Some silky soft beans work well here, as do fried plantain or potatoes. A salad finishes it all off in style.

Try not to fight over who gets the tip of the picanha. It is some of the finest steak you will ever eat. See if you can get it as cook's perk.

SHREDDED BEEF

Jalisco   Serves 4–6

This is a delicious and simple dish that is fantastic with tortillas or, if you are being decadent, even added to a sharing plate of nachos. Beef flank is a fairly inexpensive cut of meat with a good amount of fat to keep it moist. It needs long, slow cooking to make it tender. You could use skirt steak if you can't get flank.

Some crunchy salad goes very well here, no matter how you choose to serve it.

1kg beef flank

500ml cold water

2 tablespoons vegetable oil

1 red pepper, diced

1 green pepper, diced

1 large onion, diced

4 cloves garlic, sliced

1 heaped tablespoon tomato purée

6 fresh tomatoes

1 bunch spring onions, sliced

½ bunch fresh coriander, chopped

sea salt and black pepper

Put the flank in a pot and season with salt and pepper. Cover with the cold water and bring the heat up to the boil. As soon as it starts to bubble, turn the heat down and simmer for about 2 hours. Once it is soft and tender, remove the beef from the stock and allow it to cool. Bring the stock to a fast boil, reduce it by about half and then set it aside.

Heat the vegetable oil in a large pan and soften the peppers and onion over a low heat, making sure they don't colour. Add the garlic and the tomato purée and cook it all for 10 minutes.

Score the top and bottom of the tomatoes with a sharp knife and plunge them into boiling water for 60 seconds. Remove from the water and peel the skins off. Chop the tomatoes roughly and add the onions and peppers along with the spring onions. Cover the vegetables with 200ml of the reduced beef stock and simmer on a low heat for about 10 minutes.

While the vegetables are cooking, use your clean hands to shred the cooled beef. It will pull apart into tender strands. Add the beef to the cooked vegetables and simmer everything for another 10 minutes so that the sauce thickens slightly. Stir in the coriander, season it all and serve.

Brixton stockists note: you can buy flank steak at Carniceria Los Andes.

SPICY BEEF

Senzala   **Serves 4**

This is a very tasty and easy filling for your galette (see page 114), giving a Brazilian feel to a French classic.

500g minced lean beef

1 tablespoon vegetable oil

200g fresh tomatoes

150g red pepper, diced

50g red chilli peppers, chopped

salt and black pepper

Cook the beef with the oil in a hot pan for about 15 minutes or until browned.

Skin the tomatoes by cutting a cross into the top and bottom and pouring boiling water over them. The skins will shrink back and can be peeled off. Dice them, removing the seeds.

Add the tomatoes and red peppers to the pan, seasoning to taste. Cook for another 10 minutes until the peppers are softened and the tomatoes are beginning to cook down.

Stir in the chopped chilli peppers (leave the seeds in if you like your dish hot) and simmer everything for another 20 minutes. The beef will be tender and the vegetables will be soft and juicy. Serve in a crêpe or galette.

SUYA (NIGERIAN SPICY KEBABS)

Inspired by Viva Afro-Caribbean Food Store   Serves 4

Pretty much every cuisine has a version of meat on a stick, allowing meat to be cooked quickly and to have huge amounts of flavour added to it. West African cuisine is no exception: Nigerians know it as *suya* and Ghanaians call it *chichinga*.

Here, thinly sliced meat is threaded onto skewers, rubbed with a spice mix called *tankora* (which generally includes chilli powder, cayenne pepper, white pepper, ground cloves, mace, ginger and ground peanuts) before being grilled. *Tankora* doesn't keep very well, so it's best to make it fresh each time.

Use good quality meat for this as you aren't cooking it for long and want it to be tender.

For the tankora:

50g ground peanuts or whole unroasted peanuts

2 teaspoons red chilli powder

2 teaspoons cayenne pepper (reduce this if you prefer less heat)

2 teaspoons ground white pepper

2 teaspoons onion powder

2 teaspoons garlic powder

2 teaspoons sea salt

1 teaspoon ground ginger

1 teaspoon ground cloves

1 teaspoon ground mace

If you can't get ready-ground peanuts, grind the whole peanuts in a coffee grinder or pestle and mortar. You want to keep them as dry as possible rather than blending them until they resemble peanut butter. I like to buy unroasted ones with skins on for this. Omit the salt from the recipe if you can only get salted peanuts.

Spread the ground peanuts on a baking tray and place them in a low oven (about 50°C) for 8 hours or overnight if possible, to dry them out.

Mix all the remaining spices with the ground peanuts and set aside.

For the suya:

750g sirloin steak, thinly sliced

1 tablespoon vegetable oil

6 tablespoons tankora

½ white cabbage, finely shredded

4 ripe tomatoes, sliced

2 onions, finely sliced and tossed in lime juice

10–12 wooden skewers

The easiest way to slice sirloin for this is to put it in the freezer for 15 minutes to firm up, and then cut thin slices against the grain. Serve 2–3 skewers per person.

Soak the skewers in cold water for 30 minutes. Toss the sliced sirloin in the oil to coat it.

Put the *tankora* in a zip lock bag and drop in half the sliced sirloin. Shake the bag until everything is well coated and then thread the meat onto your wooden skewers with the meat flat – almost as if you are sewing through it. Repeat with the remaining meat. This is your *suya*.

Grill the *suya* under a hot grill or over charcoal for 2 minutes each side and serve with the cabbage, tomatoes and onions, and some extra *tankora* on the side for dipping. This is a spicy dish and goes well with a cold beer.

Brixton stockists note: if you are in Brixton buy the ground peanuts from the Viva Afro-Caribbean Food Store on 3rd Avenue. They come in foil pouches. Sadly your average supermarket doesn't tend to stock them.

JERK CHICKEN

Fish, Wings & Tings   **Serves 8**

Jerk chicken is probably the dish most people associate with Caribbean cuisine. The name comes from both the method of cooking on a barbecue known as a jerk drum and the actual seasoning itself. Everyone has a different recipe but allspice and scotch bonnet peppers are essential.

You can jerk pork or fish or even tofu, but chicken is the classic. Cook it on the bone to keep it tender and allow the skin to crisp up. Traditionally served with rice and peas and hot sauce on the side, you'll soon see why it's so popular.

2 large whole chickens, cut in quarters

1 tablespoon sea salt

1 tablespoon garlic powder

2 scotch bonnet peppers, whole

1 large white onion, peeled and roughly chopped

15 cloves garlic, peeled

2 bunches spring onions, roughly chopped

50g fresh thyme

2 tablespoons annatto oil (see recipe on page 122)

2 tablespoons dark soy sauce

2 teaspoons ground allspice

1 teaspoon coarsely ground black pepper

Rub the chicken quarters with the salt and garlic powder. When you quarter a chicken it combines breast and leg meat for the best of both worlds.

To make the jerk seasoning paste, combine all the remaining ingredients in a food processor or pestle and mortar and blend until well combined. Spread the paste over the chicken pieces and marinate for at least 3 hours or overnight.

Preheat the oven to 220°C. Place the chicken in a roasting tin and roast for 30–40 minutes or until the skin is crisp and the juices run clear. Serve with rice and peas (see page 115) or Trinidadian dumplings (see page 113).

You can also cook the chicken outside on a barbecue which will enhance the flavour. Use a mixture of charcoal and wood chips you've soaked in water to get lots of smoke going, giving it an authentic Jamaican taste.

JOLLOF RICE

MTK African Restaurant   **Serves 4**

Jollof rice probably needs little introduction. It is the dish everyone associates with West African, and particularly Nigerian, cooking. Thick with tomatoes, spiced with peppers and usually cooked with chicken, it is the ultimate one pot meal. A pot of jollof rice makes any get-together a party...

The secret is to use fresh tomatoes rather than tinned, and to wash the rice well to remove the starch before parboiling it. This allows the grains to stay separate as they cook. Don't worry if the rice catches a bit on the bottom of the pan: this is not only normal, but the bottom-of-the-pot, or *socarrat*, is seen as the best bit of the dish and is highly prized. For vegetarians, omit the chicken and dried crayfish and use a good vegetable stock.

500g long-grain rice

3 tablespoons vegetable or palm oil

4–6 chicken thighs, skin on and bones in

6 large fresh tomatoes

2 scotch bonnet peppers

1 large onion

3 spring onions

1 red pepper

1 tablespoon dried crayfish (or 2 anchovies)

1 teaspoon smoked paprika

½ teaspoon ground allspice

½ teaspoon ground ginger

½ teaspoon ground nutmeg

1 tablespoon fresh thyme leaves

1 tablespoon tomato purée

800ml chicken stock

salt and black pepper

Start by washing your rice well in cold water until the water runs clear and any starch has washed away.

Drain the rice, and put it in a large pot. Cover with about four times as much cold water and bring to the boil. Cook until the rice is just tender and a grain can be cut in half between your fingernails (this will take about 7 minutes). Drain the rice in a sieve and plunge it into cold water to cool. Drain again and set aside until needed.

Season the skin of the chicken with salt and pepper. Heat 2 tablespoons of the oil in a large pan and brown the chicken for 2 minutes each side. You want the skin to be crispy and brown. Remove the chicken from the heat and set on a plate.

Skin your tomatoes by cutting a cross in the top and the bottom, pouring boiling water over them and leaving for 30 seconds. Lift them out of the water and the skins should peel away easily. Roughly chop the tomatoes. Finely chop one of the scotch bonnets, discarding the seeds. Dice the onion and slice the spring onions. Chop the red pepper. Put all the chopped vegetables into a blender and blend them until you have a smooth paste.

Heat the remaining tablespoon of oil in the pan you cooked the chicken in and fry the dried crayfish and the ground spices for 1 minute. Add the tomato and pepper paste and cook for 4–5 minutes. Add the thyme and the tomato purée. Season it all well with salt and pepper and cook for another 2 minutes until it is bubbling.

Carefully stir in the drained rice so each grain is well coated in the tomato mix. Put the chicken pieces on top, skin side down, and add the remaining whole scotch bonnet pepper to infuse its flavour. Gently pour in the stock. Allow the pot to come to the boil, cover with a lid and then reduce the heat so the stock simmers.

Cook for 15–20 minutes or until the stock is all absorbed. If your pan doesn't have a glass lid that allows you to see in the pan during cooking, cover the rice with a sheet of greaseproof paper once it comes to the boil. This allows you to lift the lid and press the paper with a spoon to check for liquid without losing all the vital steam in the rice.

Once the stock is absorbed, take the pan off the heat and leave it to sit for 10 minutes with the lid still on to allow the rice to steam further. This makes the rice fluffier and makes it easier to spoon out the *socarrat* or bottom-of-the-pot. It also rests the chicken to make it even more tender.

Serve spoonfuls of the rice (including the bottom-of-the-pot) in a bowl with a piece of chicken per person. You should have enough rice for the inevitable request for seconds.

SANCOCHO DE GALLINA (COLOMBIAN CHICKEN SOUP)

El Rancho de Lalo   Serves 4

Sancocho is a soup/stew that is very popular in Colombia. The texture is loose like soup but with the depth of a stew. It is made with fresh sweetcorn, a staple food in Colombia, and the spicing comes from a paste called *aliños* which is made from peppers, cumin, garlic and achiote. This version is best using a boiling hen, but you can use a chicken instead. *Sancocho* is often eaten alongside rice which you dip into the soup as you eat.

1 large whole chicken, jointed in 4 or 8 pieces

3 litres cold water

120ml aliños paste (see page 127)

2 green plantains, peeled and cut into 5cm pieces

6 medium-sized potatoes, peeled and halved

450g frozen or fresh yuca (cassava), in chunks

3 cobs sweetcorn, cut into thirds

¼ bunch fresh coriander, chopped

salt and black pepper

Put your jointed chicken in a large pot, cover with the cold water and bring to the boil. Turn the heat down immediately until the water barely blips and simmer for about 40 minutes.

Stir in the *aliños* paste, green plantains and a teaspoon of salt. Skim any froth from the surface of the stock that occurs at this stage. Cover and cook for another 30–40 minutes, keeping the heat low.

Add the potatoes, yuca, corn and plenty of black pepper, and continue to cook everything for 30 minutes or so, until the yuca and potatoes are tender when a fork is inserted into them. Stir in the fresh coriander.

Serve the *sancocho* in shallow soup bowls, with boiled rice on the side if you like. Make sure each bowl contains both chicken and vegetables. Eat the chicken from the bone and the corn straight from the cob – don't be afraid to use your hands!

Brixton stockists note: if you'd like to try using the boiling hen, you can get one at Dombey Meats in neighbouring Market Row. The frozen yuca is available from the Faiz Food Store on 1st Avenue.

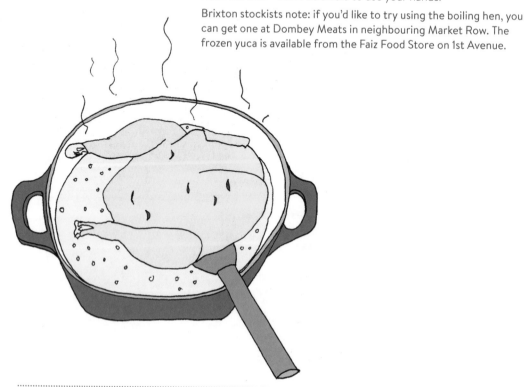

GANG KEAW WARN GAI
(THAI GREEN CURRY WITH CHICKEN)

Kaosarn   Serves 4

....

This curry is one of the signature dishes at Kaosarn. It works equally well with tofu and can be made vegetarian by omitting the fish sauce and chicken stock. You can make the paste in advance to make this a great week-night dinner everyone loves.

50g green curry paste (see page 128)

2 tablespoons vegetable oil

400ml Thai coconut milk

300g chicken breast, thinly sliced

100ml chicken stock or hot water

1 tablespoon palm sugar

2 tablespoons Thai fish sauce

100g aubergine, cut into 1cm pieces

100g bamboo shoots, cut into 1cm pieces

25g Thai pea aubergines

4 kaffir lime leaves, torn into pieces

12–15 Thai sweet basil leaves

2–3 long red chillies, cut into strips

Heat the oil in a wok or large frying pan. Add the green curry paste and 2 tablespoons of the coconut milk and cook over a medium heat, stirring until the oil and green curry paste combine and turn green. This prevents the paste separating later on.

Add the sliced chicken and stir well to coat it in the paste. Keep stirring over a medium heat until the chicken begins to colour on the outside. Pour in the rest of the coconut milk and the chicken stock or hot water, then increase the heat and bring it to the boil. Add the palm sugar and fish sauce and stir until the palm sugar melts into the curry.

Put the aubergines, bamboo shoots and pea aubergines into the curry, then reduce the heat to medium and simmer for 8–10 minutes.

Finally, stir in the torn kaffir lime leaves and the sweet basil. Scatter with strips of red chilli and serve with rice.

Brixton stockists note: do look for Thai coconut milk if you can. It is very thick, almost like coconut cream, but smooth and velvety. Aroy-D is the best and most widely available brand. Make sure you don't buy coconut milk that has cornflour in it to thicken it. The Wing Tai Oriental Supermarket stocks Aroy-D.

You can buy pea aubergines at the Kumasi Market on 3rd Avenue

CURRY GOAT

Fish, Wings & Tings

Serves 4–6

Curry goat is a real Caribbean favourite and is excellent with roti or the traditional roast bread on page 111 to soak up all the juices and flavours. Goat is a delicious meat which tastes like a slightly gamier version of lamb. It takes strong flavours well and becomes very tender when slow cooked. If you can't find it you can use lamb, but it will break down quicker during cooking so adjust the time accordingly.

1kg goat, preferably leg

5 cloves garlic, chopped

1 lime, juiced

1 teaspoon ground cumin

1 tablespoon madras curry powder, mild or hot depending on your taste

1 scotch bonnet pepper

2 tablespoons vegetable oil

1 large onion, chopped

1 litre chicken stock

salt and black pepper

Ask the butcher to dice the goat into medium-sized (3–4cm) chunks for you.

Marinate the goat in the garlic, lime juice, cumin and curry powder for 24 hours. If you want a bit of heat in the dish, chop your scotch bonnet pepper and add it to the marinade. Otherwise, keep it whole and add it later when the stock goes in.

When you're ready to cook the goat, heat the vegetable oil over a medium heat and soften the onion for about 10 minutes. Add the marinated goat and cook, stirring, for about 15 minutes to brown the meat and intensify all the flavours. Depending on the age of the goat, it may give off some liquid at this stage.

Pour the stock over the meat, making sure you have enough to cook it without the pan drying out and catching – top up with water if needed. Bring everything to the boil, then reduce the heat and cover the pan. Simmer for around 2 hours or until the meat is soft and tender.

Serve with the pumpkin stew on page 101, spiced chickpeas on page 108 and green snake beans (*bodi*) for a real taste of Trinidad, and enjoy.

Brixton stockists note: I like to get my goat at PJ Horwoods on 1st Avenue near the Pope's Road entrance. They have the most flavoursome goat around.

ROAST LAMB WITH SALSA VERDE

Casa Sibilla   Serves 4

This is Paola's signature dish. Use the best quality British lamb you can and let the flavours of this simple dish stand out. Perfect for sitting down at a table with friends and family to share and savour it, this dish sums up the ethos of Casa Sibilla perfectly.

You could substitute potatoes for the Jerusalem artichokes if they're not in season. Do try and use the onion squash: some supermarkets and vegetable box schemes keep a great range through the autumn and winter, but if you can't find it then any small winter squash will work.

For the lamb:

2 rumps of lamb, with the fat on (total weight about 600g)

2 tablespoons fresh rosemary, finely chopped

4 cloves garlic

130ml olive oil

100ml white wine

1 onion squash, peeled, halved and seeds removed

3 carrots, peeled and halved

6 Jerusalem artichokes, peeled and quartered

For the salsa verde:

4 tablespoons fresh parsley, finely chopped

1 tablespoon olive oil

1½ cloves garlic, chopped

1 tablespoon capers, chopped

1 slice soft white bread, crusts removed

1 hard boiled egg yolk, finely chopped

3 anchovy fillets, chopped

1 tablespoon red wine vinegar

1 tablespoon Dijon mustard

Marinate the lamb in a bowl with the rosemary, one finely sliced clove of garlic, 50ml of the olive oil and all the white wine for at least 12 hours to fully infuse the flavours.

When the lamb has marinated, preheat the oven to 200°C. Heat a further 2 tablespoons of the olive oil in a large roasting tin in the oven for a few minutes, and then toss the squash, carrots and Jerusalem artichokes in the warm oil. Add the three remaining cloves of garlic, peeled but left whole, and roast in the oven for 45 minutes.

Meanwhile, cook the lamb. Lift it out of the marinade and pat it dry; then season it well. Heat the remaining 50ml of olive oil in a very hot frying pan and seal the meat on all sides. You will need to do each piece individually to prevent overcrowding and the meat steaming instead. Put the browned rumps in a roasting dish.

Turn the oven down to 190°C and put the lamb in to cook for 10–15 minutes. Your lamb will be medium with the centre still quite pink (the best way to serve it). Keep the vegetables in the oven while the lamb is cooking.

Remove the lamb from the oven and leave it to rest for a few minutes. Slice each rump into three pieces. Take the vegetables out when the lamb is ready.

To make the salsa verde, chop the parsley really finely and put it in a bowl with enough oil to stop it browning. Pound up the garlic, capers, bread, egg yolk and anchovies with the red wine vinegar using a pestle and mortar. Add to the chopped parsley and mix everything well, and stir in the Dijon mustard to taste. Season the salsa verde carefully as the anchovies and capers are quite salty.

Serve the lamb with the roasted vegetables and a good spoonful of the salsa verde on top of it.

NKATENKWAN (GHANAIAN GROUNDNUT STEW)

Inspired by Kumasi Market   **Serves 4**

This is a classic dish in Ghana. Meat, fish and vegetables are cooked in a groundnut paste which thickens as it cooks and keeps the meat and fish very moist and almost buttery. The groundnut paste makes this very filling and means you can use no meat at all if you prefer. You can make it thick like a stew and serve over rice, or add more water to make it a soup which is a great way to use up any leftovers.

Groundnut paste is smoother than peanut butter and has palm oil in it for a traditional West African flavour. If you can't find it, you could use smooth sugar-free peanut butter and add a larger pinch of smoked paprika. Any meat will work; I just happen to love mutton's flavour here.

500g mutton or chicken thighs

1 tablespoon vegetable or palm oil

6 shallots, chopped

2 medium onions, chopped

4 cloves garlic, chopped

1 red pepper, diced

1 tablespoon smoked paprika

1 teaspoon cayenne pepper

1 tablespoon ground ginger

1 scotch bonnet pepper

250g groundnut paste

200g pumpkin, peeled and chopped

8 pods okra, chopped

1 x 400g tin chopped tomatoes

1 tablespoon ground crayfish (or 3 anchovy fillets)

2 cobs sweetcorn, each chopped in 4 pieces

250g white fish, such as pollock or tilapia

½ bunch fresh coriander to serve

salt and black pepper

Ask your butcher to cut the mutton into medium chunks. If you are using chicken thighs, remove the skin and the bones and cut each thigh into quarters. Tie the bones together with string in a bundle and reserve. Season the meat.

Using a very large saucepan you can cook the whole dish in, seal the meat in the vegetable oil over a medium heat (you might have to do this in batches). Set aside once it's browned. Soften the chopped shallots, onions and garlic on a low heat in the same pan – don't let them colour or burn. Add the red pepper and cook for another 5 minutes, stirring in the paprika, cayenne and ginger about a minute before the end. If you want your soup spicy, chop the scotch bonnet in here too.

While the vegetables are softening, put the groundnut paste in a small pan and add 500ml of cold water, stirring over a medium heat until it is smooth and easy to pour. It may look at one point as if it is about to split, don't worry – it comes back together. Bring the mixture to the boil, stirring until it coats the back of your spoon and the natural oils rise to the top.

Add the meat back to the softened vegetables along with the pumpkin and okra. Mix well to coat everything with the spices. Put in the bunch of tied chicken bones (if using), then pour in the chopped tomatoes and stir everything well. Scatter the ground crayfish over it all. These are widely used in West African cooking to give a savoury base note – just as Europeans use anchovies. They dissolve into the sauce and add flavour.

Pour over the groundnut paste mixture and add another 1½ litres of cold water, stirring well. If you didn't chop in the scotch bonnet earlier, pop the whole pepper into the pan now. Bring everything to the boil, then lower the heat and simmer, covered, for 2½ hours, checking to make sure the soup isn't getting too thick. If it looks like it is drying out, add a little more water.

After this time, add the corn on the cob and the white fish. Check the water level and cook it all for another 30–45 minutes, until the corn is tender and the fish is flaking apart. I like to use a thick fillet of white fish here, skinned and pin boned, but you could also use whole tilapia or something meaty like conger eel steaks. Don't use cod, which is overwhelmed by the taste of the groundnuts.

Serve this, scattered with chopped fresh coriander, in deep bowls either with rice or as a soup with *gari* or *eba*.

Brixton stockists note: buy the groundnut paste in the Kumasi Market on 3rd Avenue. You can get the *gari* there too. I bought the ground crayfish in the Viva Afro-Caribbean Food Store on the same avenue.

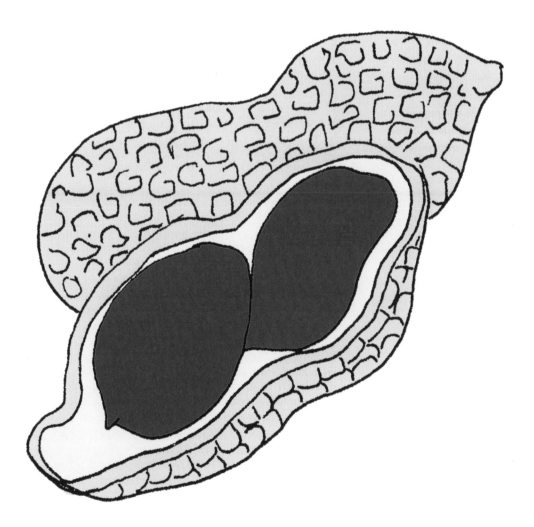

HAM HOCK AND PARSLEY TERRINE

Cornercopia   Serves 4–6

This is a classic English dish. It is well worth the time and effort, especially if you are a confident cook. It is perfect on a warm summer's day as a cold lunch.

You should be able to get ham hocks from all good non-halal butchers. The pigs' trotters are used to flavour and enhance the gelatine around the meat, but aren't eaten. Try to use leaves of gelatine for this recipe: it is known as 'silver gelatine' and has a firmer set than the powdered version. It is usually available in the baking section of any supermarket.

1 ham hock, preferably smoked (about 1kg)

2 pigs' trotters, scrubbed clean

1 good handful of parsley (about half a large bunch)

1 large carrot, peeled

1 bay leaf

2 cloves

1 strip of lemon peel

250ml good quality dry cider

2 large or 4 small shallots, peeled and left whole

2 teaspoons wholegrain mustard

2 leaves silver or leaf gelatine

Soak the ham hock overnight in cold water to remove any excess salt.

The next day place the hock and pigs trotters in a pot and just cover with cold water. Bring to the boil for 4 or 5 minutes, simmer for the same time again, and then drain and rinse in fresh cold water.

Pick the parsley leaves off the stalks and set aside 50g of them. Reserve the stalks.

Now, once again, put the drained hock and trotters in a large pan or stockpot and this time add the parsley stalks, whole carrot, bay leaf, cloves, lemon peel and half of the cider. Then top up the pot with cold water until the ingredients are just covered and bring to a steady simmer for 3–3½ hours. Add water as necessary and, from time to time, remove any scum that appears with a slotted spoon.

Add the whole shallots when you have about an hour left of cooking time, to keep them relatively firm.

When the meat is falling away from the bone, turn off the heat and let everything cool down in the pan for 30 minutes. Remove the hock, shallots and carrots with a slotted spoon and place them on a tray to cool down further. Do not discard the stock.

Using very clean or, better still, gloved hands remove all the cooled meat from the bones, keeping it fairly chunky. Discard any sinew, veins or gristle along with the trotters themselves. Dice the carrots and shallots and add to the meat.

Blanch the picked parsley leaves in boiling water for 20 seconds, refresh in iced water, and drain and squeeze them well until all the liquid is gone (this will keep their colour). Chop the parsley leaves finely and toss with the meat, carrots and shallots. Mix in the mustard, together with 100ml of the reserved stock.

Pass the rest of the stock through a fine strainer or muslin cloth into a clean pan. Boil hard to reduce until you only have around 350ml left, and then stir in the remaining cider. You will need to skim any froth from the stock, or you can strain it again through a second piece of clean muslin or a fine sieve.

Bring the stock to a simmer. Meanwhile soak the gelatine leaves in a little cold water until softened. Squeeze out any excess water and stir them into the stock with a whisk until they melt. Take your stock off the heat at this point as overcooking the gelatine stops it setting. Let it cool for 15 minutes or so.

Line a 2lb loaf tin or terrine mould with food-grade cling film. This will make it easier to remove the terrine for serving and is much less stressful than shaking the tin or dipping it into hot water to loosen it. Set the tin on a tray. Fill with the meat mixture, levelling it off neatly, and then carefully pour in the gelatine stock until the tin is well filled (you may not need it all). Place the tray in the fridge overnight to set.

Unmould the terrine and enjoy in slices with cornichons, hot mustard and a glass of vintage cider.

Brixton stockists note: Dombey Meats in neighbouring Market Row will order the smoked ham hocks for you. The silver gelatine is available in the A&C Continental Deli on Atlantic Road.

BARBECUE RIBS

Brixton Village Grill   **Serves 4 as a main**

Marinate these pork ribs for as long as possible and then make sure the meat is cooked until it's meltingly tender before rolling up your sleeves and getting stuck in. Kids love them and leave clean bones and clean plates behind, even if their faces and hands aren't!

These ribs are great with a salad full of juicy tomatoes, crisp lettuce and a sliver or two of red onion. They are sublime with the hand cut chips that the Brixton Village Grill team prepare daily. No wonder people invite themselves to Cidalia's house every time she cooks...

4 cloves garlic

a generous handful fresh coriander, roughly chopped

1 tablespoon smoked paprika

500ml white wine or vermouth

1.5kg pork ribs (allow 5 per person)

salt and black pepper

In a pestle and mortar, crush the garlic, coriander and paprika, seasoning well with salt and black pepper. Add the wine and pour over the ribs. Allow them to marinate for at least 30 minutes, but up to two days, in the fridge for the most flavoursome meat possible.

The best way to cook these ribs is to barbecue them over charcoal for tender meat and a delicious smokiness. Wait until the flames have died down and the coals glow white (it may be easier to do them as racks of ribs). Cook the ribs for about 15–20 minutes or until they're starting to crisp round the edges.

If you don't have a barbecue, these grill beautifully. Get the grill as hot as possible and cook the ribs for 15 minutes, turning them at least once. Serve piping hot.

MISO BUTA SOBORO (MINCED PORK WITH MISO)

Okan   **Serves 4 as a side dish**

Miso buta soboro is designed as an *otsumami* or side dish like the recipes on page 92. It is excellent served on top of steamed rice with freshly cut spring onions, or served on top of the *yaki-nasu* (grilled aubergines) on page 96.

200g minced pork

3 tablespoons grated ginger

2 tablespoons miso

2 tablespoons brown sugar

6 tablespoons kaeshi (see page 132)

pinch of sea salt

Mix all the ingredients together well and then brown them gently in a large frying pan until the meat is cooked and crumbles nicely. Scatter on the dish of your choice.

Brixton stockists note: Brixton Wholefoods on Atlantic Road sells a variety of miso. Use a brown version here, not the lighter white kind.

MOO-PING (CHARGRILLED PORK ON SKEWERS)

Kaosarn **Makes 12 skewers**

You can use an inexpensive cut like pork shoulder for this. To get thin slices, pop the meat in the freezer for about 15 minutes before cutting, as it firms it up and makes it easier to slice without tearing.

4 tablespoons light soy sauce

1 tablespoon dark soy sauce

2 tablespoons fish sauce

4 tablespoons palm sugar, grated

4 stems coriander root, chopped

1 tablespoon ground white pepper

2 cloves garlic, chopped

6 tablespoons vegetable oil

1kg pork shoulder, thinly sliced

Put all the ingredients except the pork in the blender and blend until you have a smoothish paste. Pour this over the pork slices and marinate for at least 2–3 hours (or overnight, if possible) to allow the flavours to develop.

About 30 minutes before you want to make the *moo-ping*, soak 12 wooden skewers in cold water and take the pork out of the fridge to come to room temperature. Then start skewering the pork, making sure the pieces are all flat on one side. Leave enough space on the skewers at the top to allow you to hold them.

Grill your *moo-ping* over hot coals or under the hottest grill you can get until they are cooked through and starting to char at the edges. This should take about 5 minutes each side.

Serve with the roasted chilli sauce on page 124.

Brixton stockists note: Brixton Wholefoods on Atlantic Road stocks a range of soy sauces. You can buy the palm sugar in the Faiz Food Store on 1st Avenue.

PORK SCRATCHINGS WITH LIME, CHILLI AND SALT

Inspired by Carniceria Los Andes   Serves 4 with drinks

People often think of pork scratchings as a traditionally British thing served with pints of mild in a pub with an open fire, but they are actually widely eaten worldwide. They are especially popular in South and Central America where they are known as *chicharrón*. In Colombia, they form the basis of a meal rather than just being a snack. When I saw that Carniceria Los Andes in the Village sells pork skin, I knew that I had to try mixing the two styles to create the ultimate scratchings... You may think a kilogram of pork skin sounds like a lot, but the skin reduces in size as you cook it, and these are so delicious you'll want extra. Any pink or purple markings on the skin are harmless.

1kg pork skin

2 teaspoons white or malt vinegar

2 tablespoons sea salt

juice and zest of 2 limes

1 teaspoon *shichimi tōgarashi* or red chilli flakes

Ask your butcher to cut the skin into long strips about 3cm wide. If you want to use the scratchings for dipping, leave them like this. Otherwise, cut them into squares of about 3cm.

Wrap the skin in kitchen paper or a tea towel for an hour to absorb any excess moisture. Then lay the pieces on a chopping board and brush the upper side only with the vinegar. If you do this with the cut pieces, it crisps the edges more than doing it in one piece. Rub with a tablespoon of the sea salt and leave them, uncovered, in the fridge overnight.

The next day, preheat the oven to 160°C and place the pork skin on a rack above a deep roasting tin, to catch the fat as it renders out. Cook the scratchings for an hour at this low heat, checking halfway through. You will be amazed by how much fat drains out of them at this stage.

After an hour, turn the heat up to 220°C and roast the scratchings for about 10–15 minutes, checking to make sure they don't burn. They should be golden brown and nicely puffed up at this stage. Remove them from the oven and allow to cool.

While the scratchings are cooking, zest or grate the limes onto a microwave-safe plate. Dry the zest out in the microwave in 20 second bursts until it is powdery but not yellowed. This took about 1 minute 40 seconds for me.

When the scratchings have cooled for about 5 minutes, spritz them with the lime juice and then sprinkle the lime zest, chilli flakes and remaining sea salt on them so that it all sticks to the skin.

Leave the house or distract yourself well for the next 45 minutes or so to allow the scratchings to cool completely so that you aren't tempted to start snacking on them until they are crisped and crunchy. Your will-power will be tested to the limits at this stage.

If you don't devour all of these in one sitting with a cold crisp beer and good company, they will keep for several days in an airtight container.

COLOMBIAN SLOW-COOKED PORK

Inspired by the Colombian cuisine in Brixton Village   Serves 4–6

This slow-cooked pork is inspired by the cuisine at Restaurante Santafereño and El Rancho de Lalo and made possible because La Carniceria Los Andes does plump juicy hands of pork at a fantastic price. It is marinated for up to 48 hours with cumin and coriander and a Caribbean-coast twist of scotch bonnet and thyme. Cooked for at least 8 hours, it is soft and meltingly tender either as a main course or as delicious leftovers on tortillas or *arepas*.

½ pod alligator pepper (optional)

1 tablespoon coriander seeds

1 scotch bonnet pepper, chopped and seeds left in

2 tablespoons smoked paprika

4 sprigs fresh thyme, leaves only

2 tablespoons ground cumin

½ bunch fresh coriander, roughly chopped

3 cloves garlic, roughly chopped

1 teaspoon sea salt

juice of 2 limes

1 tablespoon liquid smoke (optional)

1.5kg hand of pork

Make the rich smoky marinade by grinding the alligator pepper and coriander seeds in a mortar and pestle, and then adding in the chopped scotch bonnet pepper, smoked paprika, fresh thyme, cumin, fresh coriander, garlic, salt, lime juice and liquid smoke (if using), ingredient by ingredient, until you have a soft paste. Or use a hand blender and blitz all the ingredients together at once.

Pierce the pork all over with a skewer and then rub the marinade into the meat well. Make sure to wear latex gloves so you don't end up with anything going numb when you touch the scotch bonnet. Leave the pork in the fridge for up to 48 hours to let all the flavours really soak in.

Preheat the oven to 220°C and put the pork in a roasting tin on a rack or trivet. Roast for about 40 minutes so that the skin and outside is well browned. Then take the meat out and reduce the oven temperature to 130°C. While the oven cools, cover the pork with a tent of foil so that it will steam and roast at the same time.

Return the pork to the oven and cook it for 6–7 hours (overnight is best) or until the meat is soft and tender. A little longer won't ruin it. Take it out of the oven and pour the juices off carefully into a jug. Shred the pork with two forks and serve with the juices poured over.

Whether you eat it as a Sunday lunch, piled on tortillas or *arepas*, or in a sandwich, it is particularly good with hot salsa like the ones both Restaurante Santafereño and El Rancho de Lalo serve. See page 126 for a great version.

Brixton stockists note: you can buy the liquid smoke in the Faiz Food Store on 1st Avenue. It is excellent in any marinade or any food you'd like to add a barbecued flavour to.

ROAST PORK

Fish, Wings & Tings

Serves 4–6

This makes a fantastic Sunday lunch or centrepiece for a family party. Very simple but packed with flavour, it will become a favourite in no time. In Trinidad, pork is a mainstay at Christmas and is always served with hot pepper sauce. The garlic mellows as you roast it so don't be alarmed by the quantities. This dish could be made even tastier by cooking it outside on a wood or charcoal grill.

1kg fresh boneless pork belly, skin left on and scored

8cm piece of ginger

25 cloves garlic, peeled and grated

1 tablespoon fresh thyme leaves

2 scotch bonnet peppers, finely chopped

375ml dark rum

10–15 dashes Angostura bitters

2 tablespoons annatto oil (see page 122)

sea salt and freshly ground black pepper

Ask your butcher to score the skin on the pork or use a super sharp knife to do this yourself. Place the pork in a dish and season well.

Finely grate the ginger and then squeeze the pulp over a small bowl to extract the juice. Discard the pulp. Add all the remaining ingredients to the juice and mix; then pour the marinade over the meat. Massage it into the pork (it is best to wear gloves for this if you are sensitive to chilli) and leave it to marinate overnight in the fridge.

Preheat the oven to 250°C and take the pork out of the fridge to come up to room temperature. Line a roasting tin with foil and place the pork in it, scraping off any excess marinade.

Roast the pork for 1 hour, then remove from the oven and allow to cool. Cut the pork into cubes and serve with hot pepper sauce on the side. The skin will be crisp and the meat very tender.

Brixton stockists note: you'll get beautiful pork belly from Carniceria Los Andes.

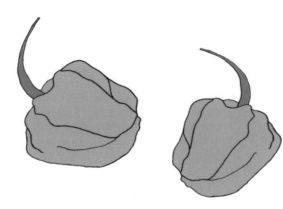

DUCK EGG SCOTCH EGGS

Snugg   Makes 6

Duck eggs are larger than a hen's egg with a creamier yolk. They go beautifully with sausages or black pudding, and a shallow-fried Scotch egg like this is just the way to introduce them. These make a great snack with a beer or cocktail or will make your co-workers envious of your packed lunch.

Use good quality ingredients here. The sausages should be made from well-seasoned pork without extra flavourings. The breadcrumbs must come from good stale bread or you could buy quality white or panko breadcrumbs. Avoid those canisters of golden breadcrumbs. A little treat like a duck egg needs respect.

6 duck eggs

8 pork sausages, skinned

150g plain flour, seasoned

2 hens' eggs, beaten

150g breadcrumbs

250ml vegetable oil for frying

Start by soft boiling your eggs. Pour boiling water from a kettle into a medium saucepan and bring it back up to a rolling boil. Lower the eggs in carefully and boil for 6½ minutes. Remove the eggs from the boiling water immediately and plunge into ice cold water to stop them cooking any further. The yolks should be slightly soft inside but the whites firm enough to handle. Let them cool and then peel them carefully.

Skin the sausages and break the meat up a bit. Make sure it is well chilled before you wrap it round the eggs or it will split and expose the egg (I keep it in the fridge until needed). Set out everything you need to coat the eggs before you start. Put the seasoned flour in one bowl, the beaten egg in another one next to it and, finally, the breadcrumbs in a third.

Pour the oil into a high-sided frying pan to a depth of about 4cm and allow it to heat up over a medium heat while you wrap the eggs. Don't use olive oil. It has too strong a flavour, and it won't get hot enough so the eggs will end up soggy.

Dab your clean hands in flour and lift a handful of sausage-meat. Make a flat burger-like patty about the size of the palm of your hand and fold it over the cooled egg, aiming to cover it completely. You can patch with extra meat, but it's better to cover it in one go if you can. Each egg takes a little bit more than one sausage so you will need all eight. Once the egg is wrapped in sausage-meat, roll it in the seasoned flour and tap any excess off. Dip it in the beaten egg and then roll in the breadcrumbs, covering it all well. Shake any excess off. Set on a plate. Repeat until all six eggs are wrapped, dipped, crumbed and ready.

Check your oil. If it is shimmering rather than bubbling, lower the eggs in carefully. Do three at a time so as not to overcrowd the pan and make the eggs greasy. The eggs should be about three-quarters covered in oil. Fry the eggs on each side for 4–5 minutes, turning them gently with a slotted spoon or tongs. The breadcrumbs should be golden brown. If the oil is too hot, take the eggs out and reduce the heat slightly before continuing. Remove the eggs from the pan with a slotted spoon and drain on kitchen roll.

Repeat with the remaining eggs. Eat warm with mustard or tomato chutney on page 137 or serve cold with the condiment and cocktail of your choice. Try not to drip the perfectly soft yolk on your chin...

Brixton stockists note: you can buy six duck eggs in The Duck Egg Café on Coldharbour Lane.

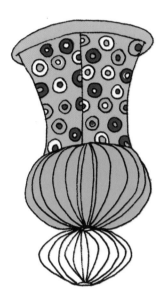

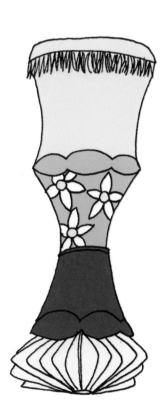

POMEGRANATE-GLAZED AFRICAN LAND SNAILS

Inspired by Viva Afro-Caribbean Food Store   Serves 4

One of the most famous sights of summertime in Brixton Village is the baskets of African land snails outside the Nigerian-run shops. Snails are as much a delicacy in Nigeria as they are in France, and one buys them alive and fresh in the market before cleaning, preparing and cooking them at home, usually in a spicy pepper sauce.

Consider them somewhere between mussels and squid in texture and looks. Fellow gardeners who know the havoc a hungry mollusc can wreak are not likely to be sentimental about cooking them. The shell alone of an African land snail can grow up to 20cm long and, because they are hermaphrodites, one snail can hatch around a thousand offspring a year. It has traditionally made sense to protect your crops by enjoying the high protein meat snails produce.

The snails are removed from their shells and cleaned with alum to remove their natural lubrication. This takes some preparation but it is very much worth it. You can buy a bag of alum with the snails, using one piece per snail. This dish balances sweet and sour flavours and makes the most of the snails' chewy meaty texture. It makes a great starter or can be scaled up to serve at a party.

8 fresh African land snails, preferably in the shell

350ml chicken stock

1 scotch bonnet pepper

2 cloves garlic, peeled but left whole

2 red onions, one sliced and one diced

1 tablespoon olive oil

½ teaspoon ground allspice

3 tablespoons pomegranate molasses

75ml water

500g cherry tomatoes, quartered

seeds of 1 pomegranate

¼ bunch fresh coriander, roughly chopped

juice of ½ lemon

salt and black pepper

First remove your snails from their shells: it is best to do this outside if possible. You may be able to ask the market trader to do it for you if you smile sweetly enough. If not, you need a heavy object like a large stone pestle or hammer to break the shells open. Wear gloves as you do this as the edges of the snail shells are very sharp. Pull the body of the snail away from the shell and then pull off the greyish inner sac so you are left with the muscly 'foot' of the snail for cooking.

Don't be worried about the slime on the snails. This is all going to be removed with the alum and, if you do get any on your hands, be reassured that it's prized worldwide for its healing and anti-aging qualities! Using a very sharp knife, cut the foot along its natural line to 'butterfly' them and then put the snails in a large pot or bowl of cold water.

Start using the alum rocks to scrub the snail meat under cold running water. Get into the hinges and the split in the foot with the corners, almost as though you are pumicing them. It seems a little odd to start with but you'll soon get into a rhythm. I cleaned each snail three times to be sure. Once each snail is slime-free, drop it into a bowl of clean cold water and soak for at least 10 minutes. Alum is perfectly safe for consumption but can taste a little bitter so this soaking is useful.

Put the scrubbed and soaked snails into a large pan with a lid, leaving them whole. Add enough stock to come about three-quarters of the way up the snails, season them and add the whole scotch bonnet, the garlic and the sliced red onions to the pan. Bring everything to the boil and then reduce the heat to a simmer. Put the lid on the pan and braise the snails for at least 2 hours, checking to make sure the pan hasn't cooked dry. If the snails look like they are catching on the bottom of the pan, add a little bit more stock. When the snails are easily pierced with a fork they are ready. If your snails are larger, it may take closer to 3 hours to achieve this. Take the pan off the heat and set aside.

When the snails are ready, heat the olive oil in a frying pan with a lid. Cook half the diced onion until it's softened but not coloured. Keep the other half aside for the salad. Add the allspice and cook it out slightly. If the garlic from the braising pot hasn't completely fallen apart, include this too. Slice the snails into thirds or quarters, depending on size, and add them along with the pomegranate molasses. Stir the snails to make sure they're well coated, and then add 75ml of water. Put the lid on the pan and cook for 4–5 minutes on a medium heat or until the molasses has thickened to make a glaze.

Take the snails off the heat and allow them to rest while you make a salad of the quartered cherry tomatoes, the remaining diced red onion, pomegranate seeds and chopped coriander. Mix the cooked snails through, and then season with lemon juice, salt and pepper and serve. Some chopped red chilli or hot sauce works well with this dish too.

Brixton stockists note: I bought the snails at Viva Afro-Caribbean Food Store on 3rd Avenue. They are often outside in baskets, but if you don't see them do ask inside. Don't forget to pick up some alum at the same time.

The pomegranate molasses came from the Nour Cash & Carry in neighbouring Market Row where they have a huge selection.

FISH

ACKEE AND SALTFISH

Etta's Seafood Kitchen

Serves 4 as a starter or side dish

Ackee and saltfish is regarded as the national dish of Jamaica. It's often eaten for Sunday breakfast but is so delicious you can eat it any time. The ackee is a tree fruit related to the lychee, but is used as a vegetable. It has a light texture similar to scrambled eggs and works well with something solid and starchy. It is usually fairly easy to find tinned ackee in the UK.

Saltfish can be salt cod or salted pollock. You can use either, but, even if you use pollock, the dish is always known as 'ackee and saltfish'.

250g saltfish

1 x 540g tin ackee

1 teaspoon vegetable oil

1 medium onion, diced

1 scotch bonnet chilli, chopped

100g fresh tomatoes

Boil the saltfish in water for about 15 minutes. Drain and rinse, then break the fish up into smaller pieces, retaining some texture. You should have removed most of the salt but still have a savoury flavour. You don't need to soak the saltfish overnight.

Drain the brine the tinned ackee comes in, then pour some fresh boiling water over them and leave for a few minutes. Heat the oil and fry the onions and chilli pepper for a few minutes. This is what Jamaicans call 'seasoning'. Drain the ackee for a second time and then add to the 'seasoning' along with the saltfish. Allow to heat through for 3–4 minutes and then add the tomatoes and cook everything for another 2–3 minutes. Both the ackee and the saltfish are cooked; you just want to warm everything to meld the flavours together. Don't stir it too much as you don't want to break up the ackee or the saltfish.

Serve the ackee and saltfish with any starchy dish of your choice. Rice and peas, bread, dumpling or hard food (plantain, green banana and yam) are all delicious.

Brixton stockists note: you can get tins of ackee in the Faiz Food Store in 1st Avenue. It will be behind the counter so you might need to ask for it.

CODFISH FRITTERS

Fish, Wings & Tings

Serves 6

These fritters use salt cod rather than fresh, and its texture helps make these little bites so light and ethereal they've been described as being 'like a high five from Jesus'. Do make the ginger and lime aioli on page 129 to accompany them: you'll want to drink it from the bowl it's so good!

350g salt cod

1 large onion

1 bunch spring onions

1–2 scotch bonnet or habanero peppers

375g self-raising flour

1½ teaspoons baking powder

1 heaped teaspoon caster sugar

1 teaspoon sea salt

750ml water

1 litre vegetable oil for frying

Soak the salt cod overnight, changing the water at least once. Then drain the salt cod, place it in a dish and cover with boiling water from a kettle. Leave it for 15 minutes to rehydrate and cool. Strain the fish and set aside without flaking it. This keeps the fritters lighter.

Peel and dice the onion. Finely chop the spring onions and the chilli peppers, leaving the seeds in if you like more of a kick, discarding them otherwise.

In a large bowl, mix the flour, baking powder, sugar and sea salt together and then stir in the salt cod, onions, peppers and spring onions. Gradually add the water, breaking up the fish as you go so you have no clumps. The consistency of the batter should be thick, but it should still slip through your fingers when held in your hands.

Put the vegetable oil in a deep saucepan and heat to 75–80°C or until a small piece of bread starts to fry as soon as you drop it in. Slightly wet your hands, take up a handful of the batter and simply pinch off small balls of the mix. Taking care not to burn yourself, drop the balls into the oil and fry for a few minutes until the fritters are golden brown and cooked in the middle. Using a slotted spoon, remove them from oil and drain on paper towels.

Arrange five or six fritters on each plate and serve with the ginger and lime aioli on page 129.

Brixton stockists note: I buy the salt cod by the weight from Ilias' Fish.

FISH SOUP

Etta's Seafood Kitchen   Serves 4

This is a beautiful pale green soup, thick with fresh fish and vegetables, perfect for any weather. Don't be put off by the idea of using green bananas in soup: they add a creaminess you wouldn't expect. Pick the greenest, least ripe ones you can find, which should crack when you open them. Don't use plantains instead. The *cho cho* is also known as *christophene* and it has a fresh crisp flavour like a crunchy courgette. You could substitute potato if you can't find it.

This soup is very quick and easy to make and is packed with fresh healthy flavours. It's my favourite dish at Etta's.

2 carrots

2 green bananas

1 cho cho

200g calabaza pumpkin or butternut squash

200g white yam (optional)

100g okra

1 tablespoon vegetable oil

2 spring onions, chopped

4 cloves garlic, peeled and chopped

4 sprigs fresh thyme

1 scotch bonnet, whole

500ml fish stock

1 salmon fish head (optional)

1kg fish (I like red bream or snapper)

500g seafood of your choice (such as mussels, prawns, cockles or clams)

Start by preparing your vegetables. I peel them all, except the okra. It is easiest to do the bananas with an actual vegetable peeler and I do them last as they exude a sticky sap that coats your hands. Chop the carrots, green bananas, cho cho, pumpkin and yam to the same size of dice – about 2cm. Cut the okra into 1cm thick slices – you want them to collapse down to thicken the soup.

In a pan large enough for the finished soup, heat the vegetable oil over a medium heat and add the spring onions, garlic, thyme and whole scotch bonnet pepper to make the 'seasoning'. Cook this until softened, and then stir in the okra and heat it through for a minute or two. Add the rest of the vegetables and sweat, covered, for 5 minutes. Pour in the fish stock and just enough water to cover all the vegetables: this is a hearty thick soup so don't use too much liquid. If you are using the fish head, put it in now to boost the flavour of the soup. Bring to the boil, cover with a lid and reduce the heat to a simmer for 20–30 minutes.

When all the vegetables are tender, add the fish. Get the fishmonger to cut it into steaks so it is still on the bone but skinless. Put the lid back on and cook the soup for another 10–15 minutes or until the fish is starting to flake. Set the fish to one side and smash the vegetables until the soup is thick and creamy but not a purée, using a potato masher or spoon. Return the fish to the pan. If you are using prawns, add them now and leave to cook over a very low heat for 5 minutes or until they turn pink.

Meanwhile, cook whatever shellfish you are using. I soak it in cold water while everything else cooks: if any shells open at this stage, discard them as they are unsafe to eat. Put the shellfish in a saucepan with about 3 tablespoons of water, cover with a lid and cook for 3–4 minutes over a medium heat, shaking the pan from time to time. The shells should have opened and given off a small amount of cooking liquor – discard any that haven't opened.

Serve the soup in shallow bowls and top with the freshly cooked shellfish, including any cooking liquor. It's delicious with Etta's Jamaican dumplings (see page 112) on the side.

Brixton stockists note: I can buy everything for this soup at Ilias' Fish on 1st Avenue and Phil's Fruit + Veg next door, making it an easy Saturday soup.

PORCINI SOUP WITH FARRO AND MUSSELS

Casa Sibilla Serves 4–6

This is a beautiful autumn soup for when the nights start to get chilly. Farro is the grain of a specific species of wheat, but the name is sometimes used interchangeably for barley or spelt as well. Particularly popular in Italy, it is shaped like rice and has a nutty flavour. You should be able to find it in Italian delis, but if you can't get it you could use pearl barley instead.

Likewise, if you can't get the porcini mushrooms, use half chestnut mushrooms and half fresh shiitake mushrooms to give a similar taste and texture.

250g farro

6 small fresh porcini mushrooms

6 tablespoons extra virgin olive oil

2 small onions, finely chopped

2 celery stalks, finely chopped

2 garlic cloves, peeled and chopped

100ml white wine, preferably Trebbiano

2 litres boiling water

4 teaspoons double concentrated tomato purée

2 sprigs rosemary, finely chopped

1.5kg fresh mussels, scrubbed and beards removed

15g unsalted butter

½ bunch flat leaf parsley

salt and black pepper

Bring a large pot of salted water to a boil. Add the farro and cook for around 18 minutes until al dente. Drain and spread on a large plate to cool.

Trim the porcini mushrooms and cut the stems from the caps. Dice the stems and slice the caps thickly.

Heat 2 tablespoons of the olive oil in a large pot over a medium high heat. Add the onion, celery and half of the garlic. Reduce the heat to medium and cook for about 10 minutes until softened, stirring frequently. Stir in the farro. Cook it for another minute and then add 2 tablespoons of the wine and cook until it has evaporated. Add the boiling water and tomato purée. Stir to combine, bring to the boil, and then take the pan off the heat and cover to keep it warm.

Heat 2 tablespoons of the olive oil in a large non-stick sauté pan over a medium-high heat. Add the mushroom caps and stems, the remaining garlic, the rosemary and a pinch of salt and pepper. Cook the mushrooms until they are golden. Add the mushroom stems to the soup and transfer the caps to a plate.

Put the remaining 2 tablespoons of oil in the sauté pan over a high heat. Throw in the mussels and the other 70ml of wine and season. Cover the pan and cook until the mussels just open. Transfer the opened mussels to a bowl and pour the liquid from the pan into the soup.

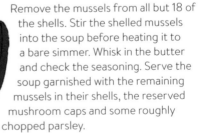

Remove the mussels from all but 18 of the shells. Stir the shelled mussels into the soup before heating it to a bare simmer. Whisk in the butter and check the seasoning. Serve the soup garnished with the remaining mussels in their shells, the reserved mushroom caps and some roughly chopped parsley.

Brixton stockists note: Farro is available from the deli at Casa Sibilla.

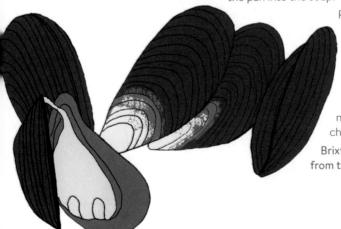

BARBECUED MACKEREL WITH AMALFI LEMON AND ROSEMARY

Casa Sibilla   Serves 4

Mackerel is an underrated fish. Not only does it have beautiful markings, it's inexpensive and abundant. The oily flesh is very good for us and it takes strong flavours well. Amalfi lemons come from the south coast of Italy and are the finest lemons in the world. If you can't get them, use good quality unwaxed organic lemons instead.

4 fresh whole mackerel, gutted and washed

4 bay leaves

4 sprigs fresh rosemary

8 sprigs fresh thyme

2 garlic cloves, peeled and sliced

1 fresh red chilli, finely chopped

2 Amalfi lemons, sliced

2 tablespoons extra virgin olive oil

1 teaspoon smoked paprika

salt and black pepper

Light your barbecue, allowing the coals to become white and covered with a fine layer of ash. If you don't have a barbecue or the weather isn't good enough, heat the oven to 180°C.

Lay your mackerel on a large baking tray and stuff the cavity of each with a bay leaf, a sprig of rosemary, two sprigs of thyme, some sliced garlic and fresh chilli and about three slices of Amalfi lemon.

Rub the skin of the fish with the extra virgin olive oil and season it with salt, pepper and a dusting of the smoked paprika.

If you are barbecuing, carefully put the fish directly on the grill and cook for 5 minutes on each side or until the skin is golden. Otherwise, put the fish on their baking tray in the oven and cook for 12 minutes.

Serve with a salad of baby leaves and tomatoes with a balsamic dressing.

BRIXTON FISH PIE WITH EDDOES

Inspired by the fishmongers of Brixton Village
Serves 4–6

Brixton Village is blessed with two excellent fishmongers, Ilias' Fish (formerly Dagon's) and L & J Fishmongers. This market has long been associated with fish and people come from far and wide to buy wet fish and seafood here. Not only is the fish always incredibly fresh, but there is also a wonderful selection.

I often make fish pie to show this catch off to friends more used to supermarket counter fish. Over the years, the recipe has evolved to this version made with fresh, salt and smoked fish, a topping of mashed eddoes and potatoes and a light, yet rich sauce flavoured with palm wine. I enjoy spending an afternoon making it and everyone always asks for seconds.

100g salt cod

200g raw prawns, shells removed and reserved

250g white fish such as pollock, coley or cod (bones reserved if possible)

2 fish heads, split

¼ bunch parsley, stalks removed and reserved and leaves roughly chopped

600ml cold water

350g smoked haddock (or any smoked white fish)

500g eddoes

500g potatoes

100g butter

2 anchovies, chopped (or 2 tablespoons ground crayfish)

50g plain flour

150ml milk

100ml palm wine (or vermouth)

50g capers (optional)

salt and black pepper

Start by soaking your salt cod. Soak it in cold water overnight, changing the water at least once, or pour boiling water over it and leave for 30 minutes.

Now make your fish stock. Use the prawn shells, any bones from the white fish and the fish heads. Add the stalks from your parsley. Cover it all with the water and bring to the boil. Turn the heat down immediately and simmer for 25–30 minutes, skimming any froth from the surface. It should reduce down to about 500ml.

Once the fish stock is ready, strain it through a sieve to remove any debris. Set the fish heads to one side and, once they're cool enough to handle, remove any flesh. Pour the stock back into a pan and lower both the white and smoked fish into it. Poach on a low heat for 5–7 minutes and then remove the fish carefully. Reserve the stock.

Flake the cooked fish into a large bowl and add any flesh from the fish head. Drain the salt cod and flake it apart with your fingers. Combine with the cooked fish, then toss the peeled prawns in and season.

Peel the eddoes and potatoes and cut them into even chunks. Put them in a pan, cover with cold water, and then bring to the boil, cooking them for about 10–15 minutes or until tender.

Meanwhile, melt half of the butter in a medium saucepan and add the chopped anchovies. Cook for a minute or two, then stir in the flour and cook for 1–2 minutes more to make a roux. Pour in 100ml of the milk, stirring constantly, and then the palm wine, and then the fish stock in increments. Keep stirring all the time and you should end up with a smooth creamy white sauce.

Add the white sauce to the bowl of fish and mix gently, tossing in the chopped parsley and capers (if using) too. Pour the whole lot into an ovenproof serving dish. Preheat the oven to 200°C.

Drain the potatoes and eddoes and allow them to sit and dry off for a minute or two in a sieve or colander. Tip them back into the pan and mash well until almost smooth. Heat the remaining 50ml of milk and beat it into the mash with 25g of the butter (hot milk makes the mash creamier than cold). Beat the mash until smooth and then spoon and spread it over the fish so it's completely covered. Run the tines of a fork over the mash to create ridges and dot the top with the remaining butter.

Bake in the oven for 30 minutes or until the topping is crisp on the top of the ridges and round the edges. Serve the fish pie with wilted greens.

Brixton stockists note: you can buy palm wine in House of Bottles on Coldharbour Lane or the Viva Afro-Caribbean Food Store on 3rd Avenue. The ground crayfish can be bought there too.

SEA BREAM CEVICHE

Inspired by L & J Fishmongers   Serves 4

Sometimes you need some crunch and citrus on your plate to freshen the palate. Ceviche is the perfect answer to this craving. A style of 'cooking' fish in citrus juice that's particularly popular in South America, it's a great way to show off very fresh fish. It's very quick and easy to make, especially if you ask the fishmonger to fillet and skin the fish for you. As it's best with white fish, I usually buy sea bream from L & J Fishmongers and serve it with steamed potatoes or rice. If you're brave, you can drink the leftover marinade, also known as 'tiger's milk'!

1 red onion, finely sliced

4 sea bream or bass, skinned and filleted

½ teaspoon sea salt

juice of 5 limes

juice of 2 lemons

zest of ½ lemon

1 red chilli, finely chopped

½ bunch fresh coriander, chopped

Pour boiling water over the sliced red onion, and then drop it into iced water for a few minutes. This takes the raw burn out of the onion.

Slice the fish into 3cm chunks and put it into a non-metallic bowl. Season with the salt, then add the drained red onion, citrus juices and lemon zest and leave to marinate for 10–15 minutes. The fish will turn white and opaque as the acid 'cooks' the flesh.

Scatter the chilli and coriander over the top and serve with potatoes, bread or rice.

SPICED ROAST STUFFED SNAPPER WITH OKRA

Inspired by Ilias' Fish (formerly Dagon's)   Serves 4

West Africa and the Caribbean share a love of fish. Cooked and eaten whole, the fish's head and tail are seen as delicacies. This means the fish must be very fresh and a lot of trust placed in your fishmonger, which is no problem in Brixton Village.

Recently taken over, Ilias' Fish used to be known as Dagon's, and was run for many years by the larger-than-life character of Gareth Hodges in his flat cap. He has now moved on to less fishy business, but this idea for spiced roast snapper stuffed with okra and lemon came from him. I've given it a bit of a tweak each time I've made it, but I still associate it with him.

4 snapper, gutted and cleaned

4 cloves garlic, minced

5cm fresh ginger, minced

2 teaspoons chilli flakes

4 teaspoons dried crayfish

2 lemons, zested, then sliced into 8 slices

4 teaspoons vegetable oil

8 pods okra, sliced

salt and black pepper

I use either red snapper or its more glamorous cousin, the rainbow snapper for this dish. Pick ones with bright eyes and shiny gills and ask the fishmonger to clean and descale them. Give the fish a quick rinse and then slash three or four cuts in the skin on either side of each one.

Combine the garlic, ginger, chilli, 2 teaspoons of the dried crayfish, 2 teaspoons of the lemon zest and some salt and pepper with the vegetable oil to make a paste. Rub this all over the snappers and marinate in the fridge for up to 4 hours.

Preheat the oven to 200°C. Put each fish on a large sheet of foil on a baking tray. Toss the sliced okra and whole lemon slices with the remaining dried crayfish and lemon zest and season well. Carefully stuff this into the cavity of the fish – it doesn't need to be tidy, just generously filled. Wrap the fish up neatly in the foil, making sure there are no gaps for the steam to escape out of. Repeat with each fish so you have four individual parcels.

Put your foil parcels on the baking tray into the oven, and roast for 25–30 minutes depending how large your fish is. The skin will be crisped enough to eat while the flesh is moist and flavoursome. The okra will be soft and tender.

Serve with the pickled garden eggs and cho cho on page 134.

SMOKED SALMON AND COURGETTE TART

Snugg   Serves 4–6

This is a beautiful tart with a rich savoury custard, salmon and caramelised onion in a shortcrust pastry. It makes a fantastic packed lunch, picnic centrepiece or dish to impress friends and family at the weekend. Don't be nervous around the pastry: it can sense your fear. Just relax and remember that the filling is the star of this show.

For the pastry:

170g plain flour

85g cool butter, cubed

pinch of salt

3 tablespoons cold water

1 beaten egg or milk to wash the pastry

For the filling:

1 tablespoon olive oil

2 large red onions, sliced thinly into half moons

1 tablespoon caster sugar

juice of ½ lemon

1 medium courgette, peeled into ribbons

250g smoked salmon

300ml double cream

1 bay leaf

¼ teaspoon nutmeg, freshly grated

1 teaspoon wholegrain mustard

3 egg yolks

1 whole egg, beaten

100g mascarpone cheese (optional)

23cm loose-bottomed tart tin

Start with the pastry, and make sure everything is set up and ready to use. Pastry ingredients need to be cold to get the best finish so work quickly. However, I find it is best to take the butter out of the fridge 10 minutes before you need it or you have to work it for longer and warm it up by accident. I put the water into the fridge at the same time.

Sift the flour into a large bowl and add the cubed butter and the salt. Gently rub the butter into the flour with your fingertips until it resembles fine breadcrumbs. Lift the crumbs up in the bowl and let them fall again to keep the air in the mix.

Add the water, a tablespoon at a time, scattering it over the mix evenly, and bring it all together with your hands. The dough should be firm, but not sticky. You may need a drop or two more water if it looks dry. Once the dough comes together in a lump, leaving the bowl clean around it, wrap it in cling film and chill for 30 minutes to relax the gluten and make it easier to roll out.

Preheat the oven to 190°C. Roll the dough out on a floured surface: you want a circle big enough to fit a 23cm tart tin and about 4–5mm thick. Butter and grease your tin.

Wrap the pastry round the rolling pin and lift it into the tart tin. Using your fingers, lift and press the pastry snugly into the tin. Don't trim it at this stage: pastry shrinks when cooked and, if you trim it, you risk not having enough depth for the filling. Prick the base a few times with a fork.

Line the pastry with greaseproof paper and fill it with dried rice or baking beans. Bake it 'blind' like this for about 15 minutes. The baking beans stop the pastry raising up. After 15 minutes, remove the greaseproof paper and baking beans. Brush the egg or milk over the pastry and return it to the oven for about 5–7 minutes until the pastry is lightly browned. Cool on a wire rack while you make the filling.

Reduce the oven temperature to 175°C.

Heat the olive oil in a frying pan over a low heat, then add the onions and soften until they are translucent. This should take about 10 minutes. Add the sugar and lemon juice to help the onions to caramelise and cook them out for another 20–25 minutes until they are a deep golden colour. Scatter them over the bottom of the tart case.

Turn your courgettes into ribbons using a potato peeler: this makes them look lovely and allows them to cook more easily too.

Arrange the ribbons of courgette and the slices of smoked salmon over the onions in the tart case so they are evenly distributed. Don't chop the salmon. You want bite to the tart.

Gently warm the cream in a small pan with the bay leaf, nutmeg and mustard over a low heat. Add the egg yolks one at a time, whisking them in well, and then the beaten whole egg. Whisk the mixture thoroughly and season, bearing in mind the saltiness of the fish when doing so.

Pour the custard into the tart tin. Finish with spoonfuls of the mascarpone (if using). Check you have reduced the oven temperature to 175°C and bake the tart for 30 minutes. The custard needs to set, but shouldn't scramble, so don't be tempted to overcook it. There should be the faintest wobble to the centre of the tart.

Remove the tart from the oven. Allow to cool for a minute or two and then set the tin on an upturned bowl and ease the tart out. Cool for 5 minutes and then serve warm with dressed salad leaves or potato salad. It can also be served cold at a picnic.

You could use shop bought pastry for the tart, but Ella's pastry is foolproof.

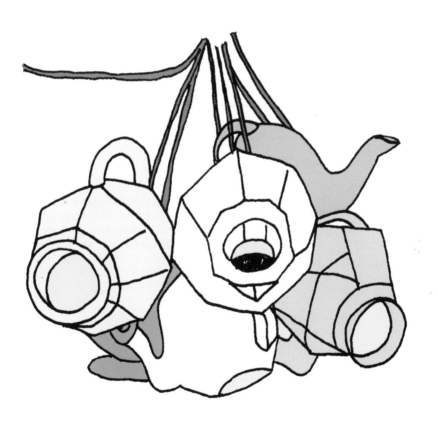

CRAB AND CALLALOO

Fish, Wings & Tings

Serves 4

Callaloo, in Brian's opinion, should be the national dish of Trinidad and Tobago because it has so much character and reflects the melting pot of people. It is a true Creole dish. Callaloo is the name of both this dish in Trinidad and a green leaf similar to spinach in Jamaica. Both like long, slow cooking.

Callaloo uses traditionally Trinidadian ingredients. *Chadon beni* is also known as Thai parsley or *culantro* and is similar to coriander in flavour. It grows as blades rather than leaves. Golden Ray margarine is beloved in Trini and has annatto for flavour and colour, but butter works just as well when mixed with the annatto oil on page 122.

2 large crabs

750g spinach or callaloo leaves

1 teaspoon white vinegar

50g butter
(or Golden Ray margarine)

2 tablespoons annatto oil

1 small onion, sliced

8 cloves garlic, chopped

5 pimento peppers, whole

2½cm ginger, peeled and chopped

1 scotch bonnet pepper, whole

15 blades chadon beni, chopped (or
½ bunch fresh coriander)

1 tablespoon fresh thyme leaves

200g salted pigs' tails (or pork ribs)

550g calabaza pumpkin, chopped
in 2.5cm chunks

24 okra, topped and tailed

1 x 440ml tin coconut milk (or milk
from 2 dried coconuts)

2 litres chicken stock

If you are using live crabs for the dish, you need to dispatch them before they go in the pot. Pop them in the freezer for about 20 minutes to make them sleepy. Then turn the crab over onto its back and look for the triangular tail piece. Lift this up and you'll see a small deep hole. Drive a metal skewer or screwdriver into this hole, giving whichever you use a good tap with a hammer so that it reaches the shell on the other side. This kills the crab instantly and painlessly. Give the crabs a good clean and set them aside.

Soak your spinach or callaloo leaves for about 10 minutes in a bowl of cold water with a teaspoon of white vinegar added. Drain and repeat until the water runs clear. This may take two or three repeat soaking and washings of 10 minutes each depending on the leaves.

In a deep pot, melt the butter and annatto oil and sauté the chopped onion, garlic, whole pimentos, ginger, chadon beni, thyme and the pigs' tails or ribs for about 2–3 minutes until everything softens slightly.

Add the pumpkin, okra and the drained spinach or callaloo leaves. Stir well. Pour in the coconut milk and the stock, place the crabs on the top and stir again. Bring to the boil, then reduce the heat and simmer for about 45–60 minutes until the pumpkin is tender. Taste and season with salt and black pepper. Remove the crabs and set them aside to cool for a few minutes. Take the pigs' tails or ribs out as well and discard – they are for flavouring more than anything else.

Blend the callaloo with an immersion blender until it is thick and glossy and serve this either in bowls as a thick soup or on rice. Joint the crabs and divide them between the portions: you may find it easier to pick the meat out of the crab and scatter it on top of the callaloo.

Brixton stockists note: you can buy the chadon beni from the Wing Tai Oriental Supermarket on Electric Avenue. You'll need a friend visiting from Trini for the Golden Ray though...

CURRIED CRAB

Fish, Wings & Tings   Serves 4

This dish was born in Trinidad's sister island of Tobago and is as beautiful as she is. Choose your crabs carefully. Ideally they should be sea crabs which are the size of your palm but you can use four larger brown crabs if you can't get them. Crabs are best bought alive, popped in the freezer to sedate them and then cooked in boiling water for 2 minutes before using in the recipe. This gives the freshest sweet flavour to the meat.

2 tablespoons vegetable oil

1 medium onion, finely chopped

6 cloves garlic, finely chopped

3cm ginger, peeled and finely chopped

1 small scotch bonnet pepper, finely chopped

4 tablespoons madras curry powder, hot or mild

8 medium sea crabs, cleaned and cut in half

1 teaspoon fresh thyme leaves

1 x 440ml tin coconut milk

1 litre fish stock

salt and black pepper

Heat the vegetable oil in a large pot and sauté the onion, garlic, ginger, scotch bonnet pepper and curry powder for 2 minutes.

Add the crabs, thyme leaves, coconut milk and about half the fish stock. Stir everything well, season and then simmer for about 30 minutes, checking the level of the stock and adding more if it looks too thick. You may not need it all.

Serve this with the Trinidadian dumplings on page 113.

WEST AFRICAN-INFLUENCED MUSSELS AND CHIPS

Inspired by Iya-Ibadan   Serves 4

Mussels are a great introduction to seafood. Easily available, simple to cook and packed with flavour – you can't ask for more from your dinner. This recipe draws inspiration from the use of tomatoes and chilli peppers in West African cooking. It has an extra depth from the fantastically named alligator pepper.

Highly prized in West Africa, especially Nigeria where the Yoruba incorporate it into naming ceremonies for babies, this pepper comes in a dry pod that looks like an alligator's back and has a warm bite of pepper mixed with a slight hint of black cardamom. (Use a mix of these if you can't get alligator pepper.) Use this recipe as an excuse to try something new and to buy one of those huge cooking pots from Bibs Konsult on the corner of 6th Avenue in the Village.

2kg mussels

4 large sweet potatoes

2 small onions, finely chopped

1 scotch bonnet pepper, finely chopped

2 teaspoons palm oil

1 pod alligator pepper

500g cherry tomatoes

125ml water

1 litre vegetable oil for frying

First clean your mussels well. Pull the beards from them and discard any that are broken or are open and don't close when tapped. Leave them to soak in cold water to clean out any grit while you turn your attention elsewhere.

Peel your sweet potatoes – I prefer the orange-fleshed ones here. Cut them into chips, making sure that they are all roughly the same size and thickness so they cook evenly.

Heat the vegetable oil to 75–80°C in a large pan. Once a cube of bread sizzles in the hot oil and turns brown without burning, it is ready for frying. Carefully drop about half the sweet potato chips in and fry for 3–4 minutes until crisp and golden. Remove the chips from the oil with a slotted spoon and drain on kitchen roll or a clean tea towel. Repeat with the rest of the chips.

While the chips are frying, finely dice the onions and the scotch bonnet pepper. Heat the palm oil in a large saucepan and soften them both in it for about 3–4 minutes. Cut the alligator pepper pod in half, scoop the seeds out and grind them in a pestle and mortar before adding to the onion and chilli to cook out slightly. Cut your tomatoes in half and add to the pan. You don't need any extra seasoning.

When the tomatoes start to collapse slightly round the edges, put the drained mussels in the pan. Pour in the water, put the lid on and cook for 3–4 minutes or until the mussels have opened and the sauce is starting to thicken. You may need a touch more water. Discard any mussels that haven't opened.

Take the pan off the heat and leave the lid on while you dish up the sweet potato fries on a separate plate. Then serve the steaming hot mussels in bowls with a good amount of the tomato-rich liquor and dig in.

The best way to eat mussels is to use an empty shell to pick the meat out of the next one. Enjoy each flavoursome mouthful as the warmth of the chilli and alligator pepper builds a tingle on your lips and the pile of shells grows. Best eaten with an ice cold beer and a roll of kitchen paper to hand.

Brixton stockists note: you can buy the alligator pepper by the pod from Iya-Ibadan on 4th Avenue.

PIRI-PIRI PRAWNS

Brixton Village Grill   Serves 4

Piri-piri peppers are a variety of bird's eye chilli pepper, packing a mighty punch despite their tiny size. Piri-piri is the Portuguese-Mozambican name for these peppers and has become the name of the recipe as well.

These prawns themselves aren't spiced but are served at Brixton Village Grill alongside liberal helpings of their piri-piri sauce. Each piri-piri sauce recipe is unique to the person who makes it and I couldn't get Cidalia to part with her version. You'll have to come down to Brixton Village Grill and try to guess how they make it so good or you can try mine on page 125.

1kg tiger prawns, shells off but tails left on

5 cloves garlic

3 tablespoons ground paprika

½ bunch fresh coriander, chopped

250ml lemon juice (approximately 4 lemons)

1 x 440ml tin coconut milk

salt and black pepper

If your tiger prawns aren't cleaned, do this by opening them down the back with a knife – just enough to remove the dark thread inside that is the digestive tract. Don't open the prawns out completely. I usually thread them onto skewers at this stage to make them easier to cook.

Make your marinade by crushing the garlic, paprika and coriander together into a paste. Season with salt and black pepper, then add the lemon juice and coconut milk and pour over the prawns, coating them well. Marinate for at least 30 minutes.

Cook the prawns under the grill for 3–4 minutes each side: they are ready when the flesh turns pink. They will be especially good if you can cook them over charcoal.

Serve with a rocket and Parmesan salad and a liberal helping of piri-piri sauce on the side.

Brixton stockists note: Ilias' Fish on 1st Avenue keep the large tiger prawns that are best for this dish.

VEGETABLES AND VEGETARIAN DISHES

FRESH COCONUT AND CUCUMBER SALAD

Inspired by the greengrocers of Brixton Village   Serves 4 as a side dish

When I was a child you only saw brown hairy coconuts at Halloween, so when I moved to Brixton I was thrilled to find you can buy them throughout the year. They are also fresher than the ones I remember, and contain a good amount of refreshing water inside which means the flesh is moist and tender. Once shelled, they can be grated for a variety of recipes. This is a light and refreshing salad, perfect in the summer or with spicy food. The coconut flesh freezes well if you want to reduce the quantities. I also use fresh coconut in my peanut and coconut cookies (page 151).

1 brown coconut

2 small cucumbers

½ red onion

½ teaspoon black mustard seeds

½ red chilli (optional)

juice of 1 lime

25g fresh coriander, chopped

Pick out a coconut that feels heavy when you shake it. Look for the three eyes at the bottom of the nut. Using a screwdriver, poke each one until one gives. Drain the water out and drink it to refresh you.

Place the coconut on the floor or a sturdy surface and tap with a hammer around the middle, rolling the coconut over so you can tap the whole way round. It will crack open more easily than you might expect. Give each half a hard tap with the hammer and the flesh will come away from the shell.

Grate the flesh on the largest holes of a box grater – you don't need to remove the thin brown outer skin. De-seed the cucumbers and dice them. Finely dice the onion and mix it all together. Stir in the black mustard seeds.

When you are ready to eat, dress the salad with the chilli, lime juice and coriander. Serve with grilled fish or the jerk chicken on page 50.

Brixton stockists note: you can buy the coconuts at any greengrocer in the market. Shake well before buying to check there's some water inside.

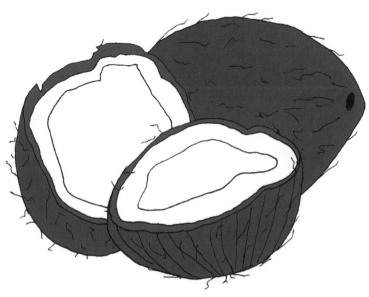

PEA, BROAD BEAN AND CURD CHEESE SALAD

Cornercopia   Serves 4 as a starter, 2 as a light lunch

This is a wonderful summer salad, bursting with the flavours of an English market garden. It makes a great light lunch or starter and goes well with a glass of elderflower cordial or sparkling wine. It's very flexible: the broad beans could be replaced with runner beans, fresh edamame beans or courgettes. Try a soft boiled egg or strained yoghurt in place of the curd cheese. If you have them available, decorate the salad with pea shoots, mustard cress or nasturtiums.

200g baby broad beans (podded weight)

200g peas (podded weight)

1 spring onion, finely sliced

1 large handful fresh herb leaves – either mint, coriander, parsley or basil

1 tablespoon grapeseed oil

juice and zest of 1 lemon

200g curd cheese, ideally goat or ewes' milk

sea salt and freshly ground black pepper

You need to double pod the broad beans, first removing the velvety outer pods and then blanching the beans to remove the tough inner skins. Blanch the beans in boiling water for 60 seconds and then plunge them into iced water to refresh them. You can then slip the skins off to reveal the jewel green beans inside. Pod the peas and blanch and refresh as above.

In a large bowl, mix the podded broad beans and peas, the sliced spring onion, and half the herbs you are using with the grapeseed oil, lemon juice and zest. Gently toss it together and season well.

Transfer the dressed salad to a serving dish. Drop spoonfuls of curd cheese on top and scatter with the remaining herbs. Serve.

Brixton stockists note: Cannon & Cannon in neighbouring Market Row have a selection of British curd cheeses with variety throughout the year depending on the season.

OTSUMAMI

Okan

The following recipes are all *otsumami*, or 'small dishes' designed to be eaten alongside any alcoholic drink, but especially beer in the summer or hot sake in winter. They have deep savoury flavours but aren't so hearty as to replace a meal. They could be described as a Japanese tapas or *pintxos*. These ones are all vegetarian, but the *miso buta soboro* on page 63 also makes a great *otsumami*.

The ingredients for all these recipes are widely available in any supermarket, as well as from many of the traders in Brixton. Moto wants to introduce simple Japanese recipes that are easy for anyone to cook, no matter where they live, and is amazed at how many Japanese ingredients you can get on any high street – even in Orkney, where her mother-in-law lives!

MOYASHI NO OSHITASHI (BEANSPROUT SALAD)

Serves 4

370g bag of beansprouts
2 tablespoons kaeshi (see page 132)
2 teaspoons sesame oil
pinch of sea salt

Simply empty the bag of bean sprouts into a pan of boiling water for a minute until slightly softened. Drain and rinse with cold water; then squeeze them to drain any excess water out. Mix in a large bowl with the *kaeshi* and sesame oil.
Serve cold.

DAIKON SALAD

Serves 4

Daikon is a Japanese radish, also known as *mooli*. It is long and white and has the pleasantly peppery flavour you associate with radish, but with a slightly earthy flavour similar to beetroot. You can use regular sesame seeds here, but Moto would always use the rounded black Japanese ones.

1 daikon (about 500g)
2 tablespoons sesame seeds
2 handfuls cress
2 tablespoons goma-dare (see page 130)

Peel the daikon and cut into long thin strips or julienne. Soak for 5 minutes in ice cold water to crisp it up and freshen the peppery flavour. While it's soaking, roast the sesame seeds in a dry pan over a medium heat.

Drain the daikon, pat dry in a cloth and put in a dish. Sprinkle with the roasted sesame seeds and the cress, and then drizzle with the *goma-dare* (sesame dressing). Serve immediately.

Brixton stockists note: you can always get daikon in the Wing Tai Oriental Supermarket on Electric Avenue.

JAPANESE POTATO SALAD

Serves 4

I adore potato salad and this is a particularly delicious version of it. The Japanese adore mayonnaise and squeeze it liberally over many dishes. Mixing it with the sesame dressing or *goma-dare* is a light, fresh use for it that is so moreish you'd be advised to double the amounts if you want to have any leftovers.

1kg salad potatoes

1 teaspoon butter

4 tablespoons plain yoghurt

4 tablespoons mayonnaise

4 tablespoons goma-dare
(see page 130)

sea salt and white pepper

You can use any potatoes for this, but it is especially good with a salad version like a Charlotte. Cut them into bite-sized pieces, leaving the skin on. Boil for about 7 minutes or until tender, but not falling apart. Drain well.

Put the potatoes back in the pan with the butter, shaking the pan until the butter is completely melted from the residual heat of the potatoes. Then put the potatoes in a bowl and toss gently with the plain yoghurt, mayonnaise and *goma-dare*. Season with salt and white pepper and serve.

TWO WAYS WITH TOFU

Japan is famed for its use of tofu, where it is not seen as a meat substitute but an ingredient in its own right. It has a clean taste that absorbs other flavours well. In Japan, there are countless varieties available, all made freshly from soya beans. In the UK, silken tofu should be easily available in any shop with a Japanese section.

HIYAYAKKO (COLD SILKEN TOFU)

Serves 4

Moto's dad enjoys this almost every day in the summer with a cold beer as a starter. It is the dish that converted me to tofu.

340g silken tofu
2 spring onions, chopped
1cm fresh ginger, peeled and grated
1 tablespoon kaeshi (see page 132)

Cut the silken tofu into 3cm cubes. Sprinkle it with the spring onion and grated ginger. Pour *kaeshi* over the top and serve.

MIZORE YU TOFU (TOFU WITH DAIKON)

Serves 4

This is a soup-like pot dish for winter. *Mizore* means sleet in Japanese and refers to the sleety scattering of daikon over the tofu and stock. It is an excellent dish for when you feel you've over-indulged or are coming down with a cold.

340g silken tofu
750ml water
1 piece dashi konbu (seaweed), chopped into 3cm squares
100g daikon, grated
1cm fresh ginger, grated
1 teaspoon chives, finely chopped
juice of 1 lime
2–3 tablespoons kaeshi (see page 132)

Cut the tofu into six cubes. In a small pan or *donabe*, gently boil the water with the *dashi konbu* for 10 minutes to create a stock. Add the tofu cubes and cook for 5 minutes, and then put the tofu and stock in a serving dish (if you have made it in a *donabe*, then you can serve it straight from the pot). Scatter with the grated daikon and sprinkle over the ginger, chives, lime juice and *kaeshi*. Serve.

YAKI-NASU (GRILLED AUBERGINE)

Serves 4

This is one of my favourite dishes at Okan and can be served hot or cold. It can be served as it is for a wonderful silky vegetarian dish or topped with *miso buta soboro* (minced pork) on page 63.

2 small (200g) or 1 large (400g) aubergine
5cm fresh ginger, peeled and grated
1 tablespoon kaeshi (see page 132)

Run a knife round the hull of the aubergine to slightly separate the green stem from the body.

Grill the aubergines whole until they are soft and wilted and the skin has blackened and blistered. Holding the top of each one with a cloth or gloves, peel while they are still hot: the skin will come away easily. Cut the aubergine into pieces and serve scattered with the grated ginger and *kaeshi*.

INGEN NO GOMAAE
(GREEN BEANS WITH SESAME DRESSING)

Serves 4

This simple dish takes green beans to a whole new level with the nutty sesame dressing. It is perfect for a packed lunch.

200g green beans
50g sesame seeds
2 tablespoons goma-dare (see page 130)

Top and tail the green beans. Boil briskly for 2–3 minutes until softened, but make sure they still squeak when you bite them. Plunge them into ice cold water for 5 minutes to keep them vividly green and crisp. Roast the sesame seeds in a dry pan over a medium heat for 3–5 minutes. Drain the beans and pat dry with a tea towel. Dress them with the *goma-dare* and roasted sesame seeds.

JAPANESE OKRA, TWO WAYS

OKURA ITAME (FRIED OKRA)

Serves 4

20 okra pods
2 tablespoons sesame oil
1 teaspoon sunflower oil
1 teaspoon shichimi tōgorashi (Japanese 7 spice powder)
1–2 tablespoons kaeshi (see page 132)
sea salt to taste

Cut the okra in half lengthwise and fry lightly in a mixture of the sesame and sunflower oils for 1–2 minutes, making sure you don't overcook it. It should still have a crunchy texture. Once the okra is lightly browned, add the *kaeshi* and a little sea salt and fry for a minute more.

Dish up and sprinkle with *shichimi tōgorashi*. Use more or less *kaeshi*, as you like.

OKURA NO AEMONO (OKRA SALAD)

Serves 4

20 okra pods
1 tablespoon white sesame seeds
1 tablespoon kaeshi (see page 132)
1 teaspoon katsuo bushi (bonito flakes)
pinch of sea salt

Slice the okra into bite-sized pieces. Toss the okra with the sesame seeds. Dress with the *kaeshi*, *katsuo bushi* and sea salt, then serve.

AUBERGINE RAGOUT

Casa Sibilla

Serves 4 as a side dish

Until Paola gave me this recipe, I couldn't cook an aubergine to save my life. Now I have them at least once a week and I've cooked this so many times I know the recipe by heart. Unlike many, Paola doesn't salt her aubergine before cooking, but cooks it for a very long time until it's absolutely soft and tender. The ragout goes beautifully with pasta or grilled meats, but I sometimes eat it just on its own drizzled with a little olive oil because it's so good. Use the best quality tomatoes you can find.

1 tablespoon olive oil plus more for drizzling

1 medium onion, finely sliced

3 cloves garlic, finely sliced

500g best quality chopped tomatoes or passata

1 large aubergine, cubed

½ bunch fresh basil

salt and black pepper

Heat the olive oil in a large pot and sweat the onions and garlic until they are translucent but not coloured.

Add the tomatoes, bring them to the boil and then stir in the cubed aubergine. Reduce the temperature to a low heat, cover the pot with a lid and simmer for 2 hours. Add a little bit of water about 75ml at a time if the sauce looks too thick or as if it will burn.

The dish is cooked when your aubergine is soft and silky. Season it with salt and freshly ground black pepper and stir in the fresh basil, roughly torn up. Drizzle with extra virgin olive oil before serving.

CARAMELISED ONIONS

Senzala   Serves 4

This is a delicious filling on its own or with goat's cheese for a fabulous vegetarian galette.

1 tablespoon olive oil
25g unsalted butter
500g red onions, sliced
150g soft brown sugar
3 tablespoons white vinegar
salt and black pepper

Heat the olive oil and butter in a large pan, then add the red onions and sweat for about 15 minutes over a medium-low heat. It should soften but not colour. Don't cover the pan or the onions will get soggy. Add the sugar and allow it to melt slightly.

Pour in the vinegar, season and cook on low with the lid on for 30 minutes until the onions are a soft sticky tangle and all the liquid has gone. Allow to cool for 5 minutes and serve on a freshly made galette from page 114.

UOVO AFFOGATO (BAKED EGGS)

Casa Sibilla
Serves 4

This is a delicious simple, healthy dinner or brunch. It's become a firm favourite with me when I need something quick and easy but with lots of flavour. Use the best eggs you can: I'm planning to try this with duck eggs next time I can get some.

4 large ripe tomatoes

125g baby spinach leaves, roughly chopped

2 garlic cloves, chopped

1 spring onion, finely chopped

1 teaspoon dried red chilli flakes

1 heaped tablespoon flat leaf parsley, chopped

2 tablespoon extra virgin olive oil

4 free range eggs

3 tablespoons wholemeal breadcrumbs

3 tablespoons grated Parmesan

15g unsalted butter

salt and black pepper

Preheat the oven to 180°C.

Score a cross in the top and the bottom of the tomatoes and put them in a bowl of boiling water for a minute. Remove them, peel the skin off and dice the flesh.

Place the spinach, garlic, spring onion, chilli, parsley and olive oil in a bowl. Add the tomatoes, season with salt and black pepper and mix everything together well.

Divide the spinach mixture between four ramekins, reserving about 4 teaspoonfuls. Pack the spinach down with the back of a spoon, then crack an egg over the top of each one and finish with a scattering of the reserved mixture. Mix the breadcrumbs and Parmesan together and sprinkle on top of the ramekins. Dot the tops with the butter and cover with foil.

Bake the ramekins in the oven for 25 minutes or until the eggs are almost set. Whip off the foil for the last 10 minutes of cooking to brown the top and serve.

Buon Appetito!

PUMPKIN STEW

Fish, Wings & Tings

This is the pumpkin stew Brian serves inside his legendary *rotis*. These buttery flatbreads are a staple in Trinidad and people spend years perfecting how to make them light and flexible enough to use as a wrap. The stew is sensational even without the *roti*. Brian often serves it with spiced chickpeas (see page 108) for a lovely meal that was recently voted one of the best vegetarian dishes in Brixton.

2 tablespoons vegetable oil

1 large onion, finely chopped

10 cloves garlic, finely chopped

1 scotch bonnet pepper

2kg calabaza pumpkin, cut into 3cm cubes

salt and black pepper

Heat the vegetable oil in a large pan over medium heat and sauté the onions, garlic and the scotch bonnet pepper. If you like a kick from chilli, chop your scotch bonnet or, if you like it milder, leave it whole to simply infuse the stew with its fruity flavour.

Once the onion and garlic are soft but not coloured, add in the pumpkin. If you are using the green-skinned calabaza pumpkin you don't need to peel it, but do remove the seeds and the pulp round them. Try and make the cubes equal sizes.

Reduce the heat under the pan and season with salt and black pepper. Cover with a lid so the pumpkin both roasts and steams in its own juices. Cook the vegetables for about 45–60 minutes, until the pumpkin is tender and most of the liquid has absorbed.

Take the pan off the heat and press the pumpkin with a potato masher: the consistency of the dish should be like a thick purée. Serve with spiced chickpeas (see page 108).

Brixton stockists note: you can buy calabaza pumpkin at any greengrocer in Brixton. You'll see wedges of it on every veg stall.

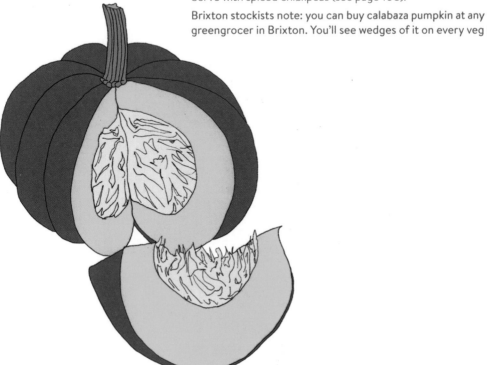

ETTA'S VEGETABLE CURRY

Etta's Seafood Kitchen   Serves 4–6

This is a simple but utterly delicious curry. Healthy, fresh and quick, it's perfect with rice and peas (see page 115). Caribbean curry differs from Indian curry in that the curry powder tends to be sweet and spicy and contain allspice rather than cardamom or mace. Coconut is also a common ingredient in Jamaican curries.

All-purpose seasoning is used widely in Caribbean cooking and is easily available. You can make your own using salt, pepper, chilli flakes, nutmeg, garlic powder, annatto, allspice, celery seed and paprika. It will store well when mixed.

200g white yam

2 sweet potatoes

250g calabaza pumpkin

2 courgettes

250g savoy cabbage

1 teaspoon coriander seeds

250g block of creamed coconut

3 sprigs fresh thyme

4 cloves garlic

2 teaspoons curry powder, mild or hot depending on preference

1 teaspoon all-purpose seasoning

1 vegetable or prawn stock cube

250–375ml cold water

Peel and chop the yam, sweet potato and pumpkin. Cut into 3cm chunks, making sure you don't keep the slightly dried ends of the yam as they can be bitter. Slice the courgettes into half moons the thickness of a pound coin, and shred the cabbage roughly.

Lightly toast the coriander seeds in a dry pan for 30 seconds, watching them closely to make sure they don't burn. This intensifies the flavour. Chop up or grate the coconut cream and put into a large saucepan with the toasted coriander seeds, thyme, garlic, curry powder and all-purpose seasoning. Add 250ml of water and put over a medium heat until the coconut cream has completely melted. Simmer for a minute or two to infuse the flavours. Reduce the heat and add the vegetables and the crumbled stock cube, along with another 125ml of water if it looks too dry. Simmer, covered, for 20–25 minutes or until the vegetables are al dente.

Serve with rice and peas and make this a weekday dinner favourite.

YAM AND DASHEEN BUTTERMILK CURRY

Inspired by the greengrocers of Brixton Village   Serves 4

Yams are a staple crop for much of the world. Not to be confused with the sweet potato, they come in a variety of sizes and colours. This dish uses white yam which you buy by the piece in the market. It has a thick skin and creamy white flesh, and when cooked it has a floury texture that soaks up flavour well.

This is a great curry: the yam is cooked in buttermilk thickened with ground peanuts, and dasheen leaves are added for colour and texture. You could just as well make it with sweet potato or squash and spinach instead, or use yoghurt instead of buttermilk. I often serve it with steamed rice.

2 tablespoons coconut or vegetable oil

1 tablespoon cumin seeds

1 teaspoon coriander seeds

1 teaspoon brown mustard seeds

1 onion, finely diced

2 cloves garlic, finely chopped

2 green chillies, chopped

500g white yam, peeled and cut into 3cm cubes

5 curry leaves

500ml buttermilk (or 450ml yoghurt and 50ml water mixed)

4 tablespoons ground peanuts

1 teaspoon sugar (optional)

300g or 2 bunches dasheen leaves, washed and roughly chopped

salt and black pepper

Heat the oil in a heavy-bottomed pan and lightly fry the cumin, coriander and mustard seeds for 30 seconds. Add in the chopped onion, garlic and chillies and cook for about 5–6 minutes until they soften. Stir in the cubed yam to coat with the spices and oil. Add the curry leaves and some salt and black pepper, and then fry it all gently for 2–3 minutes to infuse the flavours.

Pour in the buttermilk and stir for a minute or two as it warms. Sprinkle in the ground peanuts a tablespoon at a time and stir well. Do not to be tempted to add more peanuts at this stage even though it looks runny: the sauce will thicken as it cooks. Add the sugar at this point if you prefer a less sharp taste from the buttermilk.

Simmer the curry with the lid on for 10–12 minutes or until the yam can be pierced with a fork and the sauce is thick, but still spoonable. Add the chopped dasheen leaves, stir through, and cook for 1–2 minutes with the lid on until the dasheen leaves are wilted.

Serve with steamed rice or *rotis*.

Brixton stockists note: buy the ground peanuts from the Viva Afro-Caribbean Food Store. Keep them in the fridge or freezer when opened to prevent them going off. Buttermilk is available from the Nour Cash & Carry in Market Row or any grocers with a Polish dairy section.

PULSES, STAPLES AND PROVISIONS

AKARA (FRIED BEAN FRITTERS)

Inspired by Sierra Leone Groceries   Serves 4–6 as a snack

These little fritters are eaten throughout West Africa and the Caribbean and have a slightly different name in each area. Trinidadians call them 'accra' which really reminds you of their heritage. If you like falafel, you will love these. Incredibly tasty and satisfying, they are so good that during Ramadan Muslims often break their fast in the evening with them.

They use black-eyed peas which are in fact a bean. The beans are used raw in the fritters and cooked in the hot oil. You need to make the batter just before cooking to prevent it separating. Use a flavourless oil like sunflower oil to fry these rather than anything stronger like palm oil.

200g dried black-eyed peas

2 spring onions, finely sliced

1 small onion, finely diced

½ scotch bonnet pepper, finely diced

pinch of salt

2 eggs

1 litre vegetable oil for frying

Soak your black-eyed peas in cold water for at least 3 hours or overnight. Don't add any salt. Drain and rinse them with more cold water. At this stage, some cooks skin the beans by rubbing them between their palms and washing them with cold water to flush the skins out: I don't find it necessary.

Put half the soaked beans in a heavy bowl or pestle and mortar and add about 50ml of water. Blend with the pestle or an immersion blender until you get a smooth, fairly thick paste – you may need to add more water if it is too stiff. Scrape the paste into a large bowl and repeat the process with the remaining beans and another 50ml of water.

Mix the spring onions, onion and scotch bonnet pepper into the bean paste and season with a pinch of salt. Finally add the eggs to the batter, and beat for at least 2 minutes to introduce plenty of air to it.

Heat the vegetable oil to 75–80°C in a deep pan. Once a cube of bread sizzles in the hot oil and turns brown without burning, it is ready for frying. Using a tablespoon, carefully drop spoonfuls of the mixture into the oil and fry for about 60–90 seconds. Do it in batches and be careful not to overcrowd the pan. When the fritters are browned all over, remove from the oil with a slotted spoon and drain on kitchen roll or a clean tea towel.

Serve the fritters sprinkled with a bit more salt and some hot sauce on the side. They are equally good hot or cold.

Brixton stockists note: you can use bean flour in place of the raw beans to make the akara. Simply add the same weight to the batter. You can buy the bean flour at the Kumasi Market on 3rd Avenue.

FRIJOLES PAISAS (COLOMBIAN BEANS)

Restaurante Santafereño

Serves 4–6 as a side dish

South Americans can work magic with beans. Humble pulses are turned into dishes that are utterly beguiling. I love the food at Santafereño but my favourite thing is the beans. They're soft and creamy with a silky smooth sauce, and I could eat them on their own instead of just as one small part of the meal.

I had assumed they were cooked in lots of lard to get this texture, but it turns out the secret ingredient is a green plantain cooked in with them to thicken the cooking liquid and lift the flavour. Add in a *guiso* (a combination of herbs, spices and tomatoes) and these will be the best beans you ever eat.

400g dried pinto or black beans

2 pigs' tails or a ham hock (optional)

1 litre cold water

1 green plantain

For the guiso:

2 teaspoons vegetable oil

1 small onion, finely diced

2 cloves garlic, finely diced

3 spring onions, finely sliced

1 teaspoon ground cumin

½ bunch fresh coriander, chopped

1 x 400g tin chopped tomatoes

½ teaspoon salt

Soak your beans overnight in cold water. Rinse them thoroughly in more cold water as this removes a lot of the sugars that can make beans difficult to digest. Place the clean soaked beans in a large pot along with the pork (if using) and cover everything with a litre of cold water. Bring the beans to a boil, skim any froth from the surface and turn the heat down so the water moves slightly but doesn't bubble. Put a lid on the pot and cook for 2 hours. Don't add any salt at this stage as it can make the beans tough.

To make the *guiso*, heat the oil in a pan and cook the onion, garlic, spring onions, cumin and half the coriander for 5–6 minutes until softened. Add the tomatoes and the salt and cook for another 10 minutes. Set this aside until the beans are cooked. Cooking the *guiso* ahead of time intensifies the flavour.

Peel the green plantain by topping and tailing it with a knife. Then score the skin with the knife, taking care to split the skin but not the flesh inside. Remove the skin in strips and then cut the plantain into 5mm chunks.

After 2 hours, check the beans. They should have absorbed a good amount of the water and be nearly tender. Add the *guiso*, the plantain and more water if the pot looks like it will cook dry. Simmer for another 60–90 minutes, or until the beans are absolutely soft and the plantain has collapsed and thickened the cooking liquid.

Serve with rice or as part of ***bandeja paisa*** – a huge platter of food common throughout Colombia featuring beans, white rice, grilled meat, ripe plantain, avocado, ***chicharrón*** (pork scratchings), chorizo Colombiano sausage, fried egg and ***arepas*** (maize flour flatbreads).

Brixton stockists note: you can get the pigs' tails at Carniceria Los Andes on 1st Avenue or the ham hocks at Dombey Meats neighbouring Market Row.

SPICED CHICKPEAS

Fish, Wings & Tings   Serves 4

These chickpeas are fantastic on their own, but also work beautifully with the curry goat on page 108. Cooking the chickpeas this way makes them very tender, and whenever I make it everyone asks for seconds.

2 tablespoons vegetable oil

5 cloves garlic, finely chopped

1 small onion, finely chopped

1 scotch bonnet pepper

1 teaspoon madras curry powder (hot or mild depending on preference)

1 teaspoon ground cumin

3 x 400g tins chickpeas, drained

4 large potatoes, peeled and diced into 6mm chunks

1 litre cold water

salt and black pepper

Heat the vegetable oil in a large pan and sauté the garlic, onion and scotch bonnet pepper. If you like a kick from chilli, chop your scotch bonnet; otherwise leave it whole to simply infuse the stew with its fruity flavour. This is your 'seasoning' for the chickpeas.

Add the curry powder and the ground cumin to the seasoning and sauté, or *chunkay*, it all for a minute or two to intensify the flavours. Stir in the chickpeas and the diced potatoes and season well with salt and black pepper.

Pour the water over so everything is submerged, and then cook on a low heat with the lid on until the potato collapses and thickens the dish. This should take between 60–75 minutes.

Serve with curry goat (page 56), pumpkin stew (page 101), green beans and some roast bread (page 111).

TARKA DAAL
(RED SPLIT LENTILS WITH SPICED BUTTER)

Elephant   Serves 4

This is a deceptively simple dish that everyone loves. It shows just how good lentils can be. I often make it to do several meals and it never lasts as long as I think it will because I can't resist *just* one more mouthful...

For the daal:

500g red split lentils

1 teaspoon sea salt

1 teaspoon chilli powder

1 teaspoon garam masala

1 teaspoon turmeric

1 teaspoon ground black pepper

750ml cold water

For the tarka:

100g butter

2 tomatoes

2 green chillies

4 cloves garlic, peeled

5cm fresh ginger, peeled

Wash your lentils well and soak in cold water for an hour before cooking.

Put the drained lentils and the spices in a medium-sized pot and add the cold water. Bring to the boil and then simmer for an hour, adding water if it looks dry and stirring frequently.

The lentils will mush up and disintegrate into a soup. Once this happens, take off the heat and leave to one side while you start the *tarka*. This allows the lentils to thicken slightly.

Melt the butter in a frying pan over a low heat. Skin the tomatoes and cut them into small dice, and then finely chop the chillies, garlic and ginger. Fry everything gently in the butter for at least 20 minutes until the tomatoes collapse.

Stir the *tarka* into the *daal*, garnish with fresh coriander and finely sliced pieces of ginger and you have *tarka daal!*

GREEN PLANTAIN CHIPS

Inspired by Faiz Food Store

Serves 4 as a snack with drinks

Green plantains are much starchier and drier in texture than their ripe yellow cousins. The best way to think of it is that green plantain are a vegetable similar to the potato or yam. They are particularly delicious fried as a snack and are eaten this way throughout Africa and South America.

2 green plantains
¼ teaspoon cayenne pepper
salt and black pepper

1 litre vegetable oil for frying

Cut the ends off the plantains with a very sharp knife. Then run the knife down the peel from top to bottom making sure you don't score the flesh inside. Crack the peel back with your thumbs and peel it away in strips. Slice the plantains into rounds as thick as a pound coin.

Heat the vegetable oil in a deep pan to 75–80°C. Once a cube of bread sizzles in the hot oil and turns brown without burning, it is ready for frying. Carefully drop a handful of the plantains into the oil, taking care not to overcrowd the pan. Fry for about 60–90 seconds or until the plantains are golden brown.

Drain on kitchen roll or a clean tea towel and sprinkle with the cayenne pepper, sea salt and a bit of black pepper. Enjoy with a cold drink and good company.

Brixton stockists note: you can buy plantains at any greengrocer in Brixton. Buy the greenest ones you can find and store outside the fridge like you would a banana.

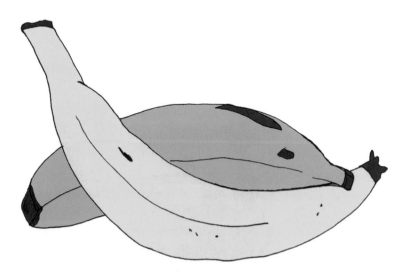

ROAST BREAD

Fish, Wings & Tings

Serves 4

This is a traditional Trinidadian side dish. You cook it in a dry frying pan and then use it to scoop up soups or stews. It is an unleavened flat bread so can be whipped up in next to no time.

500g self-raising flour
1 teaspoon sugar
1 tablespoon butter (optional)
pinch of salt
300ml water

Put the flour in a large bowl with the sugar, butter (if using) and a pinch of salt. Rub in the butter, and then gradually add about half of the water. Bring everything together with your hand, adding more water bit by bit if it looks too dry. You want a firm but not sticky dough which comes together cleanly. Set the dough aside for 15 minutes to rise slightly.

Flatten the whole ball of dough out until it is about 3cm thick. You can just use your hands to do this. Cook in a standard-sized dry frying pan or cast iron skillet you have preheated on a medium heat. Keeping it on a medium heat, it will form a crust and start to go golden brown in about 5–6 minutes.

Flip the dough over and cook the bread on the other side. If you like a softer bread, put a lid on the pan and allow the bread to steam slightly at this stage.

Serve with curry goat on page 56 or the spiced chickpeas on page 108.

JAMAICAN DUMPLING

Etta's Seafood Kitchen   Serves 4

Unlike Trinidadian dumplings, Jamaican dumplings are deep-fried and rich with butter for a light fluffiness that floats well in soup. I have to order a portion of these every time I visit Etta's.

375g self-raising flour

pinch of salt

15g butter, room temperature

½ teaspoon sugar

125ml soda water

500ml vegetable oil for deep frying

Put the flour and a pinch of salt into a bowl, and then rub in the butter with your fingertips to get a breadcrumb-like texture. Stir the sugar into the soda water and then add it to the flour a little at a time, mixing swiftly but gently with your hand until you have a firm dough. It shouldn't be sticky and "should come up bouncing", according to Etta and her cousin Carole who both make the lightest dumplings.

Knead the dough to bring it together, but don't overwork it. Then break off golf-ball-sized pieces and press a dimple into them with your thumb.

Heat the vegetable oil in a pan on a medium heat. Once a cube of bread sizzles in the hot oil and turns brown without burning, it is ready for frying. Fry the dumplings, a few at a time, for about 5–6 minutes until golden. You want them to soak up a little bit of the oil for extra flavour, but drain on kitchen roll when you lift them out of the pan.

Serve with fish soup (page 76) or ackee and saltfish (page 74), or they are delicious just on their own.

TRINIDADIAN DUMPLING

Fish, Wings & Tings

Trinidadian dumplings are boiled, unlike their Jamaican cousins. They are simple and easy to make. You can serve them with anything you fancy.

250g plain flour
1 tablespoon sugar
½ teaspoon sea salt
150ml cold water

In a bowl, mix the dry ingredients with your hand and then add water a little at a time and knead it into a soft but not sticky dough. You may not need all of the water. Using some extra flour on your work surface, roll the dough out to a 3cm thick sausage shape and then cut into 12cm lengths.

Cook in a pot of boiling water for 15 minutes before draining well. Serve with the curried crab on page 85 to soak up the beautiful curry sauce.

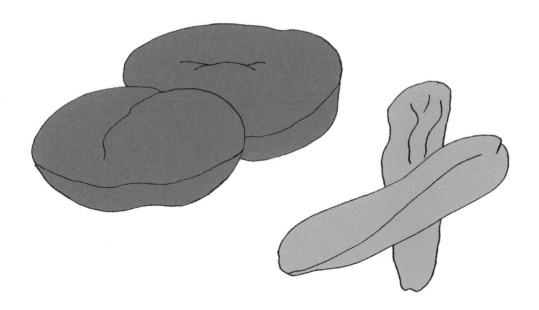

GALETTE (BUCKWHEAT CRÊPES)

Senzala

Senzala serve two types of crêpes. This one is made from buckwheat flour and is known in French as a *galette*. Buckwheat is not related to wheat and is completely gluten free: it has a slightly nutty flavour and is delicious and very easy to use. This recipe is also completely vegan.

Galettes freeze really well: just put sheets of greaseproof paper between them before you put them in the freezer. It's worth doing a big batch and having some spare this way as they are so versatile, suiting both sweet and savoury fillings and toppings. You are only limited by your imagination!

250g buckwheat flour
1 teaspoon sea salt
500ml water
vegetable oil

Simply mix the flour and salt with the water until the batter is the consistency of double cream. Chill the batter for at least 30 minutes or overnight, allowing it to come to room temperature for 15 minutes before cooking. Whisk well before using as the flour can sink slightly.

These are crêpes rather than pancakes so you want them to be very thin and easy to roll or fold. You'll need the biggest pan or skillet you have so you can spread the batter out. This will approximate the finish of using a hotplate in a crêperie. Heat the pan on a medium heat and then brush it lightly with oil. It should sizzle slightly.

You are now ready to make your galettes. Spoon about 2 tablespoons of batter into the pan and swirl it round to spread it out thinly. Allow it to cook for about a minute and then lift the edges up with a spatula. It should be golden brown and slightly bubbled and lacy around the edges.

Flip the galette over and cook for another minute on the other side. You may need to sacrifice the first one to the pancake gods as it usually takes a while to get the heat and rhythm of crêpes just right. When the galette is cooked, either fill and eat it immediately or keep it warm in the oven for a few minutes until needed. They're delicious filled with goat's cheese and caramelised onions on page 99, or with caramelised apples on page 141.

Brixton stockists note: Senzala sell high quality French buckwheat flour.

RICE AND PEAS

Etta's Seafood Kitchen

Serves 4–6

Jamaica is famed for this dish. Contrary to its name, it doesn't feature garden peas but uses pulses such as kidney beans or gungo peas. The colour of the finished dish depends on which you use: kidney beans make it brown and gungo peas more green.

This is a simple but very tasty dish, originally cooked on Sundays in Jamaica but equally delicious any day of the week.

1 x 400g tin kidney beans or gungo peas (or 250g dried)

500g rice, white or brown

250g block of creamed coconut

2 spring onions, sliced

1 clove garlic, chopped

3 sprigs fresh thyme

1 teaspoon sugar

½ teaspoon salt

1 litre cold water

1 scotch bonnet pepper, left whole

If using dried pulses, soak them overnight, then drain them and cover with fresh water in a large pan. Bring to the boil and cook for about an hour until tender, then drain. Do not add salt when boiling the pulses as this toughens them.

Wash the rice in cold water until the water runs clear: this removes the starch. Brown rice is lovely in this dish as the grains fatten up and don't stick together, but it will take slightly longer to cook.

Chop up the coconut cream and put it in a large pan with the spring onions, garlic, thyme, sugar and salt. Add 50ml of the water and put the pan over a low heat until the coconut cream has melted. Add the drained rice to the pot and pour over the remaining 950ml of water. Put in the whole scotch bonnet pepper and bring to the boil.

Cover the pan with aluminium foil and put the lid on top as well. Turn the heat down to low and cook for 30 minutes, resisting the temptation to open the foil or lid. This allows the rice to absorb the steam, and helps each grain remain separate.

Serve the rice and peas with steamed fish or curry. It is designed to be a side dish, but it always becomes the star of the show.

Brixton stockists note: every greengrocer in Brixton sells little bunches of fresh thyme because it is such a popular herb in African and Caribbean cooking.

OKONOMIYAKI
(SAVOURY JAPANESE CABBAGE PANCAKE)

Okan   Serves 1

....

Okonomiyaki means 'as you like it' and is a type of savoury pancake. Okan specialises in them and owner Moto described them to me in the terms below that can only be described as a love letter.

I grew up with this dish in Osaka.

The sweetie shop on the corner had a little griddle and they cooked a very simple *okonomiyaki* for the equivalent of 20p as a kids' snack. It was a thin batter and processed ham but with a bit of sauce it was delicious. When I invited friends over my mum always set up *okonomiyaki* at home so we could cook it ourselves from the age of 8 years old. You cook together, you eat together, you chat and share. It's the best food for that.

Okonomiyaki is a very simple recipe but each shop has a different style and taste somehow. I recently went on an *okonomiyaki* trip to Osaka to sample them. I thought I couldn't eat *okonomiyaki* every day, but I did and loved it!

There are over 3000 *okonomiyaki* shops in Osaka. When we go out for a drink, we eat at the same time and always share plates amongst friends. Osaka people love *konamon* (flour-based) foods. The character of the Osakans is different to other Japanese cities. People are very direct and not at all shy. We always talk about food, discussing where is good and cheap. It is very important to us that food is not expensive, but is good quality. If it isn't good, then your food business won't survive in Osaka. Customers are very demanding.

I left Osaka 15 years ago, but as soon as I go back and smell 'burnt sauce' in an *okonomiyaki* shop I always know I am home. I have my favourite *okonomiyaki* shops. The *obachan* (an affectionate term for an old lady) who run them always welcome me. The best shops are a bit run down and the *obachan* talk a lot and are covered with oil. Maybe that will be me one day!

Okonomiyaki are made individually to ensure freshness and that you get your personal choice of toppings. If you are cooking for more than one person, simply use the same proportions given below for each. The traditional garnishes of okonomiyaki sauce, Japanese mayonnaise, aonori (green seaweed flakes) and katsuo bushi (fermented, dried bonito flakes) can all be bought at the Japan Centre (www.japancentre.com). Moto buys her okonomiyaki sauce in and says no-one in Japan makes it themselves, but if you want to give it a go try my recipe on page 131.

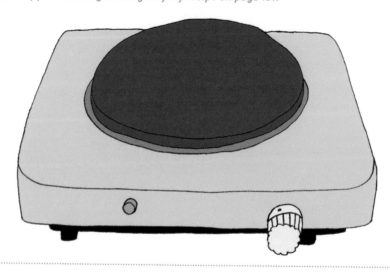

....

15g soft French yam (yamaimo), grated

40g plain flour

1 teaspoon soft brown sugar

½ teaspoon baking powder

pinch of sea salt

1 medium egg, lightly beaten

1 tablespoon stock (konbu dashi if you have it, or vegetable stock)

2 tablespoons water

120g pointed or sweetheart cabbage, finely shredded

4 spring onions, thinly sliced

1 tablespoon sunflower oil

topping of your choice (thinly sliced pork belly is traditional but unsmoked bacon works well. You can also use prawns, squid, cheese, tofu or anything you fancy. These are used raw and cooked in the process of making the okonomiyaki.)

To serve:

okonomiyaki sauce (see page 131)

aonori (green seaweed flakes)

katsuo bushi (fermented dried bonito flakes)

Japanese mayonnaise

Put the grated yam, flour, brown sugar (if you're using it) and baking powder in a bowl with a pinch of sea salt. Add the lightly beaten egg, the stock and 4–5 tablespoons of water, and fold carefully until you have a pourable batter. Do not over mix.

Heat a heavy-bottomed skillet or frying pan on a high heat for 5 minutes and then reduce it to a medium heat. While it is heating up, mix the cabbage and spring onion together in another bowl. Add enough batter to make a pourable mixture, folding carefully so as not to lose the air in it – you should have a little bit of the batter left at this stage. All the cabbage pieces should be separate from each other. It's important that you don't over mix the cabbage and batter or leave it too long: if you are making more than one *okonomiyaki*, mix each portion just before you cook it or it will get soggy.

Put the sunflower oil in the hot pan and make a mound of the cabbage batter in the middle. With a spoon, carefully make into a circle about 12cm in diameter. Arrange your toppings on the top and cook, uncovered, for about 3 minutes.

Drizzle the remaining batter over the toppings to seal them all in and then flip the *okonomiyaki* over to to cook the other side. Don't push it down. Cover the pan with a lid and cook for 5 minutes. Turn it again and cook, uncovered, for another 5 minutes.

Serve drizzled with *okonomiyaki* 'burnt' sauce, *aonori*, *katsuo bushi* and Japanese mayonnaise. If you can't get them, use crumbled nori and soy sauce instead.

Brixton stockists note: You can get *aonori* in the Oracle Juice Bar on 5th Avenue (Ita-Tunde stocks a small amount of vegan grocery items). Soft yam is widely available at any Caribbean grocery store.

YAKI ONIGIRI (FRIED RICE CAKE)

Okan

Makes 12

This is Moto's other signature dish alongside the *okonomiyaki*. She serves it from her stall at Sunday UpMarket on Brick Lane. The smell is gorgeous while it cooks. The stall is very simple, serving just *yaki onigiri* and *okonomiyaki*. It has many regular customers and Moto estimates that she has served over 100,000 rice cakes in the years she has been there. They are so good that they are one of the few reasons I leave Brixton these days…

2 tablespoons sesame oil

2 teaspoons fresh ginger, peeled and grated

100ml soy sauce

500g sushi rice

700ml water

2 tablespoons sunflower oil

Mix the sesame oil with the ginger and soy sauce in a jam jar to infuse the flavour. Set aside until later.

Rinse the rice in water three or four times, draining the water off each time. Put the rice in a 20cm heavy-bottomed pan with a tight fitting lid (like a Le Creuset pan if you have one). Add the water and leave the rice to soak for 30 minutes. Without draining, put the lid on the pot, turn the heat up to high and boil the rice for 5 minutes. Reduce the heat to low and cook for another 12 minutes.

Sushi rice is a short-grain rice that is sticky when cooked. You can tell when it is ready when you see small holes on the surface of the rice and there is no more water on the surface. Take the pan off the heat and leave it for 15 minutes with the lid still on the pan to allow the steam to absorb into the rice.

Stir the rice gently from the bottom of the pan and allow it to cool slightly (but not too much as you won't be able to shape it as easily). Put cold water in a bowl and wet your hands before shaping the rice. Form the rice into 12 small flat patties like a fishcake, each weighing 80–100g. Don't squash the rice: it should stick together easily.

Put the sunflower oil in a heavy frying pan over a medium heat. Put in the rice cakes and cook for 1–2 minutes each side until they are crispy golden brown.

Reduce the heat to low and brush the top of the rice cakes with the sesame oil, ginger and soy sauce mix two or three times, so you build up a lacquer. Flip the rice cakes so that the soy sauce caramelises slightly. If it starts to burn or get smoky, take the pan off the heat for a moment to cool.

Serve as they are or wrapped in sheets of nori.

Brixton stockists note: you can get sushi rice and nori in the Wing Tai Oriental Supermarket on Electric Avenue.

SEASONINGS

ANNATTO OIL

Fish, Wings & Tings   Makes 250ml

Annatto is a small seed also known as *achiote* and used throughout the Caribbean and Central America to flavour and colour foods. It imparts a subtle nutmeg-like taste and can be used in place of turmeric or saffron in dishes needing colour, but not as much flavour as they give.

Annatto oil is used in the marinade for jerk chicken (see page 50) and roast pork (page 67). It also makes fantastic mayonnaise.

250ml vegetable oil
(not olive or palm oil)

125g annatto seeds

Gradually heat the vegetable oil and the annatto seeds in a saucepan and simmer for about 15 minutes. Allow the oil to cool, then strain and store in a glass bottle.

Brixton stockists note: you can buy the annatto in the Nour Cash & Carry in neighbouring Market Row. It may be labelled as *achiote*.

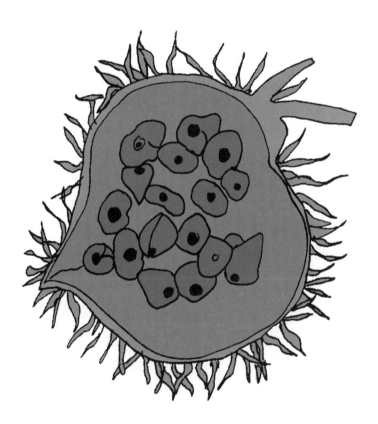

CHILLI OIL

The Agile Rabbit

Makes 250ml

A drizzle of chilli oil sets off the light, thin bases of the pizzas at The Agile Rabbit beautifully, whether you are sitting down there for the evening or simply grabbing a slice while shopping.

1 litre extra virgin olive oil

a small handful fresh green cayenne peppers

5 or so scotch bonnet peppers

3 cloves garlic, peeled

1 sprig rosemary

a bunch of thyme

1 tablespoon black molasses

Heat 5cm of the oil in a large saucepan. Meanwhile chop the cayenne peppers, scotch bonnet and the garlic and add them all to the hot oil. Add the rosemary and the thyme.

Simmer for 10–15 minutes, then add another 5cm of oil and simmer for another 10 minutes. Repeat the process until the oil is all in the pot.

Finally add the molasses and allow to simmer for a final minute or two. Take the pan off the heat and leave to cool a little before you strain the oil through a funnel into a sterilised, sealable glass bottle. Push some of the herbs into the bottle for effect.

Use on pizzas, stir-fries or salads.

ROASTED CHILLI SAUCE

Kaosarn Makes 240ml

This sauce is fantastic. Incredibly flavoursome and fiendishly hot, it is addictive... You can buy ready-ground roasted chillies and ground roasted rice in Asian supermarkets – if you can find them, use 2 tablespoons of each. Otherwise, follow the directions in the recipe to make your own.

3 tablespoons tamarind pulp, soaked (not from concentrate)

8 dried red chillies

2 tablespoons white rice

2 tablespoons palm sugar

6 tablespoons fish sauce

3 tablespoons fresh lime juice

Start with your tamarind. The stuff you prepare yourself is so much more flavoursome than the concentrate. Soak half a block of tamarind pulp in boiling water for about 15–20 minutes. Once the block has softened, take it out of the water and push it through a fine sieve with a spatula. The fibres remain behind and you have a soft thick paste left for use in the recipe.

Heat a dry frying pan. Toast your dried red chillies over a medium heat until you smell them – don't let them burn. Take them off the heat when they have crisped up and set them aside.

Using the same hot pan, toast your rice until golden brown – again, watch it like a hawk so it doesn't burn. Leave it to cool on a plate, and then grind it with the chillies in a coffee grinder or food processor.

Next, pay attention to your palm sugar. The paste version used in Thailand is best, but if you can only find a solid block you'll need to soak it before melting it. Cover about 25g palm sugar with cold water and leave for 15 minutes. Drain and put it in a pan with a tablespoon of water over a high heat, stirring until it melts.

Now all your ingredients are prepared, put them in a bowl with the fish sauce and lime juice and stir until well combined.

Serve with *moo-ping* (see page 64) – and it's also great with grilled steak. Store any excess in a sterilised jar in the fridge.

Brixton stockists note: you can buy big bags of the dried red chillies that will last ages in the Wing Tai Oriental Supermarket in Electric Avenue. You can get the palm sugar in the Nour Cash & Carry in the neighbouring Market Row.

PIRI-PIRI SAUCE

Inspired by Brixton Village Grill   Makes about 200ml

Living in Lambeth with its large Portuguese community, piri-piri sauce has become my condiment of choice. The piri-piri pepper or African bird's eye pepper has been associated with the Portuguese since around the 14th century, but it was their former colonies of Mozambique and Angola that created the marinade the whole world has fallen in love with.

6 cloves garlic, unpeeled

2 lemons

1 scotch bonnet pepper

6 piri-piri or bird's eye chillies, fresh or dried

1 teaspoon smoked paprika

1 teaspoon dried oregano

2 sprigs fresh thyme

1 teaspoon sea salt

2 tablespoons balsamic vinegar

2 tablespoons whisky (optional)

Preheat the oven to 200°C. Wrap the unpeeled cloves of garlic in foil and roast for 25 minutes. Once they're cool, squeeze out the tender insides. Zest one of the lemons and set it aside.

Remove the seeds from the scotch bonnet pepper. Put it in the blender with the piri-piri chillies, roasted garlic, lemon zest, paprika, oregano, thyme and salt and blitz until you have a thick purée.

Squeeze both the lemons, including the zested one, and add the juice to the purée along with the vinegar and the whisky (if using) to make a consistency like thick ketchup. Pour into a sterilised jar and keep in the fridge.

The piri-piri sauce can be used as a marinade on any meat or fish. It has a chilli heat which will mellow nicely when cooked. The whisky makes it a little more Portuguese than Mozambican in style, but it adds a lovely depth if you choose to use it.

Brixton stockists note: buy the dried bird's eye chillies in O Talho Portuguese Butchers on Atlantic Road. You can also get a great selection of Portuguese wines and spirits here.

AJI (COLOMBIAN SALSA)

Inspired by El Rancho de Lalo   **Makes about 250ml**

The *aji*, or salsa, served with Colombian food is so good you find yourself wanting to eat it straight off the spoon. Just hot enough to give you that desire to eat more and more, it's loaded with lots of flavour as well as heat. This version is inspired by the salsa at El Rancho de Lalo. Traditionally it would probably be made in a pestle and mortar, but I find a processor quicker and easier.

1 small red chilli or ½ scotch bonnet pepper, chopped

100ml white vinegar

½ teaspoon salt

2 spring onions, chopped

1 shallot, finely chopped

½ bunch fresh coriander, chopped

¼ bunch fresh mint, chopped

1 tomato, skinned, seeded and chopped

½ teaspoon sugar

1 lime, juiced

50ml cold water

Blend the chilli, vinegar and salt together in a food processor or large pestle and mortar. Add all the remaining ingredients and blend until you have a very loose, wet pourable sauce. Add more water if it looks too solid.

Aji goes with anything and everything but will store well in the fridge in a sterilised jar for several weeks. It is especially good with the slow-cooked pork on page 66.

ALIÑOS (COLOMBIAN SEASONING PASTE)

Inspired by El Rancho de Lalo   **Makes about 350ml**

The basis of *sancocho*, this paste features garlic, peppers, achiote and cumin. It is so popular in Colombia that you can buy shop-bought versions, but it's easy and inexpensive to make. It will keep for about a week in the fridge or can be frozen in ice cube trays to make it go further.

2 teaspoons cumin seeds

1 teaspoon coriander seeds

1 teaspoon achiote (annatto) seeds

½ green pepper

½ red pepper

½ red onion

4 spring onions

4 cloves garlic

1 teaspoon oregano, dried or fresh

1 teaspoon sea salt

1 teaspoon ground black pepper

Toast the cumin and coriander seeds in a dry pan until the fragrance is released. Remove them from the heat and grind finely in a pestle and mortar with the achiote seeds.

Chop the peppers, onion, spring onion and garlic finely. Combine with the ground spices, oregano and salt and pepper. Either use a blender or take some time with the pestle and mortar to get it as smooth as possible. Add just enough water to make the paste a dropping consistency.

You can then use the *aliños* in the *sancocho* (see page 54) or as a rub or marinade for meat and vegetables.

Brixton stockists note: the Nour Cash & Carry in neighbouring Market Row stocks achiote. Remember – as the seeds are known as *annatto* in the Caribbean, it may have either name on the package.

NAM PHRIK GANG KEAW WARN GAI (THAI GREEN CURRY PASTE)

Kaosarn   Makes about 100ml

Thai curries have become very popular in the UK and it is well worth making the paste from scratch for the extra flavour and fragrance it adds to the dish. It's still quicker than queuing for Kaosarn on a Friday night if you forget to book!

If you can't get Thai red shallots, use round pink ones instead. Don't use banana shallots. Coriander root is as it sounds and is the root of the plant. It is more robust than the leaves in cooking. You can simply buy a living pot of coriander to get them here in the UK.

20 hot green chillies

8 shallots, finely chopped

4 cloves garlic, chopped

2 stalks fresh lemongrass, chopped

5cm fresh galangal, chopped

1 tablespoon kaffir lime rinds, chopped

2 stalks coriander root, chopped

1 teaspoon white pepper

1 teaspoon sea salt

1 teaspoon shrimp paste (omit if vegetarian)

½ teaspoon coriander seeds, roasted and ground

½ teaspoon cumin seeds, roasted and ground

Put all the ingredients in the blender or pestle and mortar, blending them until you have a fine paste. You can put it in a jar and keep in the fridge for up to a month or freeze until needed.

Brixton stockists note: Kumasi Market on 3rd Avenue sell the shallots while the rest of the ingredients are available from the Wing Tai Oriental Supermarket. The lime rinds tend to be seasonal.

GINGER AND LIME AIOLI

Fish, Wings & Tings

Makes 500ml

This dipping sauce is sensational. It's fresh and tangy and just perfect with the codfish fritters on page 75. This dish was the first thing I ate at Fish, Wings & Tings and I just had to keep going back to work out what the flavours were….

500ml mayonnaise
5cm fresh ginger, peeled
1 scotch bonnet pepper
50g caster sugar
25–30ml white vinegar
juice of 1 lime

Put all the ingredients in a blender and blend until the mixture is smooth and well mixed. You want it to be a loose texture for dipping. Serve in small ramekins with the codfish fritters.

GOMA-DARE (SESAME DRESSING)

Okan

This is a super simple sesame dressing, packed with flavour. It dresses any salad or you can dip just about anything in it. It keeps well in the fridge and I've never met a vegetable it didn't enhance. You could almost eat it on its own...

2 tablespoons tahini paste

2 tablespoons soy sauce

2 tablespoons rice vinegar

2 tablespoons sesame oil

2 tablespoons honey

2 teaspoons soft brown sugar

½ teaspoon sea salt

Mix all the ingredients together well in a jam jar. If you like a thinner dressing, you can add cold water gradually, about a tablespoon at a time, until you get the consistency you like.

Store the excess in the fridge. Take it out and allow to come to room temperature before using if you can.

Brixton stockists note: If you can, use the lighter Lebanese tahini paste which is looser than many of the premium supermarket brands. Moto recommends *Al Nakhil* as a brand as the texture is most similar to Japanese sesame paste. Look for the green lid in the Nour Cash & Carry in Market Row.

OKONOMIYAKI SAUCE

Inspired by Okan

The simple charms of an okonomiyaki are turned into something special with a drizzle of okonomiyaki or 'burnt' sauce. Sweet and savoury at the same time, it's like an souped up version of HP sauce.

100ml dashi stock

5 tablespoons Worcestershire sauce

2 tablespoons tomato ketchup

2 tablespoons tomato puree

2 tablespoons dark soy sauce

1 tablespoon apple juice

1 teaspoon brown sugar

1 teaspoon honey

3 teaspoons cold water

2 teaspoons cornflour

Put all the ingredients except the water and cornflour in a saucepan and bring to the boil, stirring well to prevent it catching on the bottom of the pan.

Add the cold water to the cornflour and stir well. Add the cornflour mix a little bit at a time to the hot mixture, stirring well. Cook it all on a low heat for about 5 minutes until the cornflour has combined and the sauce has thickened to the consistency of a glossy ketchup.

Allow the sauce to cool and then transfer to a sterilised jar or glass bottle. Store in the fridge until needed.

KAESHI (JAPANESE SOY SEASONING)

Okan   Makes 700ml

This is a simple seasoning used in Japan as a base for stocks, soups, salads and noodle dishes. It uses a Japanese style of soy sauce known as *shoyu* made from both fermented soy beans and wheat. It is lighter, sweeter and more intensely savoury than Chinese soy sauce, and the two are not interchangeable. If you're not in Brixton, you can find both *shoyu* and sake in most supermarkets.

100ml sake

100g soft brown sugar

500ml shoyu soy sauce

Put the sake in a pan over a low heat until small bubbles form at the edge of the pan. Add the sugar and stir until dissolved. Pour in the soy sauce and gently bring the mixture to the boil. Remove from the heat immediately.

Allow to cool to room temperature. Pour into a sterilised bottle and keep in the fridge for up to three months until needed. It is very versatile and can be used in many recipes throughout this book.

Brixton stockists note: you can buy the **shoyu** soy sauce in Brixton Wholefoods on Atlantic Road. There is a range of sake in the Wing Tai Oriental Supermarket.

FIG RELISH

Cornercopia

Makes 4 x 300ml jars

This is the easiest relish to make. I did my first batch in under 45 minutes. Buy the best quality figs you can: Turkish or Greek ones are best and should still be slightly green in colour. The relish is especially good with soft sheep or goat's cheeses.

1kg dried figs

1 litre boiling water

500ml sherry or cider vinegar

150g unrefined soft brown sugar

1 heaped tablespoon fresh thyme leaves

2 heaped tablespoons good quality wholegrain mustard

sea salt and freshly ground black pepper

Remove the stalks from the dried figs, then put them in a pan and cover with the boiling water. Bring it back to a boil, then turn down the heat and simmer until the figs are tender, topping up the water if necessary.

Drain the softened figs, discarding the water. Put them in a deep bowl along with the vinegar and sugar, and purée them with a handblender. Take your time to catch all the figs and incorporate them fully. Stir in the thyme and mustard.

Bottle up the relish in clean jars you have sterilised for 15 minutes in a 160°C oven. The relish will keep unopened for about six months. Once it's opened, you'll eat it all in next to no time...

Brixton stockists note: I bought the figs in the Nour Cash & Carry in neighbouring Market Row. You can get beautiful sherry vinegar at the A & C Continental Deli on Atlantic Road.

PICKLED GARDEN EGGS AND CHO CHO

Inspired by Kumasi Market   Serves 4 as a side dish

This may sound like a 60s band, but it's actually a delicious and easy home pickle using African garden eggs – a kind of small white aubergine that looks like an egg. They are the reason Americans call aubergines eggplants.

Their bitter flavour is tempered here with the crisp mellow pear-like crunch of the cho cho and a variety of aromatic spices. The pickle doesn't need any complicated canning and is ready to eat in under an hour. It will keep for up to 5 days in the fridge and is fantastic with fish or steamed rice.

1 cho cho, peeled, cored and cut in eighths

4 garden eggs, sliced crossways

1 tablespoon + 1 teaspoon sea salt

250ml water

250ml rice vinegar

75g brown sugar

1 star anise pod

1 dried red chilli

1 piece fresh turmeric (optional)

½ blade mace

½ teaspoon black peppercorns

½ teaspoon alligator pepper

While you usually don't need to salt modern varieties of purple aubergines, it is advisable to salt the garden eggs for this recipe to remove any excess bitterness and to keep the slices crisp as they pickle.

Lay the slices of both the cho cho and the garden eggs on a plate and scatter them with a tablespoon of sea salt. Leave them for about 20 minutes or until you can see moisture come to the surface. Rinse the slices and pat them dry. Arrange them inside a kilner jar (or a bowl, if you're eating them immediately).

Put the water in a pan with the rice vinegar, brown sugar, 1 teaspoon of salt and the spices. If you use the fresh turmeric, it will colour the liquid. Don't reduce the salt or the pickles will go soggy. Bring it all to the boil and then reduce the volume by about half. It will become slightly syrupy.

Pour this syrupy pickling liquid, including the spices, over the slices of garden eggs and cho cho and make sure they are fully submerged. Leave for at least 30 minutes before eating. Keep the remaining pickles in the fridge and eat within 5 days.

Brixton stockists note: garden eggs are available all year at Kumasi Market on 3rd Avenue which specialises in Ghanaian foods. You can get the alligator pepper at Iya-Ibadan on 4th Avenue.

PICKLED BEETROOT

Snugg   Makes 3 x 200ml jars

If you can get a mix of colours of beetroot for this, it looks even more appetising – it is a great way to try the candy-striped or golden varieties. If you are using paler-fleshed beetroot, use white wine vinegar instead of red.

This pickle can be eaten immediately or kept for a week or two in the fridge. It goes especially well with the Scotch eggs on page 68.

400g whole beetroot

125ml red wine vinegar

125g brown sugar

125ml water

2 tablespoons coriander seeds, lightly crushed

2 cinnamon sticks

2 star anise pods

1 bay leaf

3 whole cloves

Remove any leaves or stringy roots from the beetroot and scrub them well under cold running water. Top and tail the beetroot and then boil them whole in plenty of water for 25–40 minutes, depending on their size. You want them to be fork tender but not totally cooked.

Drain the beetroot and, once cool enough to handle, peel them with a vegetable peeler. Cooking them first makes them easier to peel, although I still prefer to wear gloves to protect my hands from staining. Slice them so they are not too chunky, but hearty enough not to fall apart in the pickle. Put in a pan with the red wine vinegar, brown sugar and the water. Add the spices and bring it all to a gentle boil so the sugar dissolves.

Reduce the heat and simmer for 15–25 minutes, depending on size. You will end up with a slightly candied pickle that is a world apart from the astringent stuff you buy ready-made in jars.

Put the beetroot slices into a jar you have sterilised for 15 minutes in a 160°C oven and pour the still warm pickling liquid (including the spices) over the top. Seal the jars and store them in the fridge.

PLANTAIN CHUTNEY

Cornercopia

This is one of the easiest chutneys I've ever made and, unlike many, it doesn't fill your house with the smell of boiling vinegar. It tastes fantastic straight away, but if you do allow a month for it to mature it becomes even smoother and delicious. Ever since Iain and Anne gave me the recipe, people ask me to bring this instead of wine when I come for dinner.

Your plantains should have lots of black on the skins and the tips should be a little bit soft. I bought ripe ones and left them for four days. If you can't wait, cook yours for a little bit longer until they collapse round the edges.

175g tamarind pulp

4 small onions, peeled and finely chopped

½ tablespoon mustard oil (or sunflower oil)

1 tablespoon cumin seeds

1 tablespoon fenugreek seeds

1 tablespoon brown mustard seeds

1 tablespoon ground cinnamon

½ tablespoon yellow mustard seeds

½ tablespoon ground allspice

½ tablespoon coriander seeds

4 whole cloves

225g soft brown sugar

2 limes, juiced

6 very ripe plantains, peeled and diced into 1cm cubes

salt and black pepper

Prepare your tamarind by breaking up the block of tamarind pulp in a pan of water and bringing it to the boil. Take it off the heat and leave to soften – after 20 minutes, push the pulp through a sieve and reserve the resulting soft, smooth paste for the recipe.

Fry the onion in a little mustard oil for about 10 minutes until translucent. Add all the spices and cook through for about 2–3 minutes until fragrant. Stir in the sugar and cook gently until the sugar is melted and the onions are caramelised. This will take about 15 minutes on a low heat.

Add the tamarind paste and cook the mixture until it thickens. Add the lime juice. Finally add the plantains and simmer for 5–10 minutes. Spoon the chutney while hot into jars you've sterilised at 160°C and seal well.

This chutney will taste best if left for a month before eating. Serve with cold cuts or cheese or anything else that takes your fancy. I have made a coronation chicken with it that people loved.

Brixton stockists note: you can buy the blocks of tamarind pulp for this recipe in the Nour Cash & Carry in neighbouring Market Row.

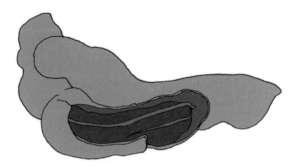

TOMATO CHUTNEY

Snugg

Makes 4 x 250ml jars

This simple chutney is a fantastic way to enjoy the flavour of summer toms all year round. It is easy to scale the recipe up or down if you want to use up a glut of tomatoes or make it to give to people. Simply use two parts sugar to one part red wine vinegar to keep the balance of sweet and sour. It can be eaten straight away or tastes delicious after it has matured slightly.

7 ripe beef tomatoes, skinned and cored

300g soft brown sugar

285ml red wine vinegar

pinch mustard powder

salt and black pepper

Use the ripest and most flavoursome tomatoes you can for this. Chop the tomatoes roughly and put them in a large pan with the sugar and red wine vinegar. Season well and add the mustard powder. Gently bring to the boil. Reduce the heat and simmer until the tomatoes collapse and the chutney becomes dark, sticky and jammy. This should take about 45–60 minutes.

Transfer the chutney while still hot into sterilised jars before sealing and keep in the fridge until needed. Serve with Scotch eggs or bacon sandwiches. It is also excellent with a mature cheddar cheese.

Brixton stockists note: you can buy big glass bottles of inexpensive but excellent quality red wine vinegar in the A & C Continental Deli on Atlantic Road. They even have beautiful labels.

SWEET THINGS

BANANA FRITTERS

Brixton Village Grill   Serves 4

You may not have had a banana fritter since the 70s, but these Brazilian-inspired ones will remind you just how good they are served piping hot with a scoop of ice cream. If you can get those small sweet finger bananas, they are even more delicious.

1 egg, beaten

4 tablespoons milk

1 teaspoon vanilla extract (or seeds of one vanilla pod)

65g plain flour

1 tablespoon caster sugar

2 teaspoons ground cinnamon

1 teaspoon baking powder

2 bananas (or 4 finger bananas)

500ml vegetable oil for frying

Mix the egg, milk and vanilla extract or seeds in one bowl and the flour, sugar, cinnamon and baking powder in another. Pour the wet ingredients into the dry and whisk to make a batter. Don't over mix it, and it is best if you allow it to rest for 10 minutes or so.

Heat the oil in a deep pan over a medium heat until it shimmers gently and a cube of bread dropped into it sizzles without burning.

Cut the bananas into quarters and coat them well in the batter. Deep fry for about 2 minutes each side until golden brown. Drain on kitchen paper and serve immediately.

Brixton stockists note: you can often get finger bananas at the branch of A & N Fresh Fruit & Veg on the corner of the Atlantic Road entrance next door to Ilias' Fish. Buy them green and let them ripen for the sweetest bananas you've ever eaten.

CARAMELISED APPLES WITH BUTTERSCOTCH SAUCE

Senzala   Serves 4

These are really easy to make and the sweet stickiness goes beautifully with the buckwheat flour of Senzala's galettes from page 114. I usually make extra as I can't resist them on porridge or muesli as well. If you are feeling extravagant, the caramelised apples go especially well with this smooth butterscotch sauce. If you have any left after a batch of galettes, it will keep well in the fridge in a jar.

For the caramelised apples:

5 apples (I like to use Braeburns)

150g golden caster sugar

2 teaspoons ground cinnamon

50g butter

Preheat the oven to 200°C. Peel and core the apples. Cut into slices as thick as a pound coin. Sprinkle with the sugar and cinnamon. Dot the butter over the slices and cook in the oven for 20–25 minutes or until the apples are sticky and golden.

For the butterscotch sauce:

Makes about 500ml

250g salted butter

250ml double cream

150g brown sugar

Melt the butter in a small pan. Add the double cream and brown sugar and heat gently. Stir the mixture as the sugar melts, being very careful in case the sauce bubbles up (it will burn!). Cook for 5–10 minutes until you have a golden sticky sauce. Serve warm.

SORBETTO ALL'ALBICOCCA (APRICOT SORBET)

Lab G   Makes 1 litre

No other country seems to have such an affinity with apricots as Italy does. Italians adore these little velvet-skinned fruits, making wonderful jams, tarts and ice creams with them. I think Italian apricots are the best in the world, but this sorbet brings the fruit to life even here in the UK.

250g sugar

500ml water

250g fresh apricots

1 egg white, lightly beaten

Prepare a sugar syrup by melting the sugar in the water on a low heat until it has dissolved and the syrup thickens. Set aside to cool.

Halve the apricots and remove the stones. Purée the halved apricots with a hand blender and then push them through a fine sieve to remove any skins.

Add the puréed apricots to the cooled sugar syrup. Pour the mixture into the ice cream machine and churn for 30 minutes. (You cannot make this sorbet to Giovanni's method without the machine. If you make it by hand, it will be a granita, which is also delicious but not as smooth.)

Add the egg white about 3–4 minutes before the end of churning to make the sorbet even smoother and help it freeze more easily. Place the sorbet in the freezer until needed or serve immediately.

SORBETTO AL LIMONE (LEMON SORBET)

Lab G

Sharp, refreshing and dairy-free, this sorbet makes a great finish to a meal. It is very easy to make and is popular with everyone.

250g sugar

300ml water

250ml lemon juice
(from approximately 6 lemons)

1 egg white, lightly beaten

In a saucepan, melt the sugar in the water on a low heat until it has dissolved. This makes a sugar syrup. Stir in the lemon juice and allow the syrup to cool.

Pour the syrup into the ice cream maker and churn for 30 minutes. (You cannot make the sorbet to Giovanni's method without the ice cream maker or it will be a rougher textured granita.)

About 3–4 minutes before the end of churning, add the egg white to help make the sorbet smoother and then freeze until needed or serve immediately.

GELATO ALLA VANIGLIA (VANILLA ICE CREAM)

Lab G   Makes 1 litre

When you taste this, you'll never again describe something dull as 'vanilla'. It's some of the best ice cream I've ever eaten...

5 medium free range egg yolks

165g caster sugar

2 vanilla pods

500ml whole milk

zest of 1 lemon

100ml double cream

This uses the same *base gelato* that the chocolate ice cream on the next page uses, but with vanilla and lemon instead of chocolate.

Prepare two bowls, a bigger one filled with ice cubes and a smaller one into which you will pour the cooked ice cream mixture. Put the small bowl inside the big one, making sure the ice surrounds it but that the inner bowl is dry, to create an ice bath. In this smaller bowl, beat the egg yolks and sugar together with a balloon whisk.

Slice the vanilla pods lengthways and scoop out the seeds with the tip of a knife. Put the seeds and pods into a saucepan with the milk and stir in the lemon zest. Over a gentle heat, bring the milk to a temperature of 85°C (just before a full simmer), but do not let it boil. Discard the vanilla pods at this point, leaving the seeds behind.

Now pour the warmed milk a little at a time onto the beaten eggs in their ice bowl, whisking quickly to prevent them from scrambling. Pour the egg and milk mix back into the saucepan and cook on a medium heat for 5–7 minutes until it thickens to a custard. Keep stirring until the custard coats the back of the spoon. You should get a silky smooth result: if you see any small lumps, it means the temperature is too high and you are overcooking the eggs. If this happens, just remove the pan from the heat and cool.

Make sure the smaller bowl is back in its ice bath and pour the custard into it. Whisk while it is cooling to keep it smooth. When it is completely cool, whip your double cream to soft peaks and then fold it into the custard with a metal spoon so you don't lose the air in it. This is your *base gelato*.

Pour it into your ice cream machine and let it do its job for around 30 minutes. If you don't have an ice cream machine, put the *base gelato* in the freezer for 6–8 hours and stir it with a fork every 30 minutes or so to stop ice crystals forming.

GELATO AL CIOCCOLATO (CHOCOLATE ICE CREAM)

Lab G

Makes about 1 litre

This is the ultimate chocolate ice cream. Dark, decadent and delicious, it isn't too sweet and is a real treat for the whole family. I enjoy it with an espresso on the side or a small liqueur for a grown-up feel.

4 medium free range egg yolks

175g caster sugar

500ml whole milk

50g dark chocolate (at least 70% cocoa solids), finely chopped

45g unsweetened cocoa powder

200ml double cream

pinch of salt

This ice cream also uses a *base gelato* like the vanilla ice cream, but omits the lemon zest and vanilla and adds two types of chocolate for luxury.

Prepare two bowls, a bigger one filled with ice cubes and a smaller one into which you will pour the cooked ice cream mixture. The small bowl needs to fit inside the bigger bowl to make an ice bath. In this smaller bowl, beat the egg yolks and the sugar together well with a balloon whisk and set it aside.

Put the milk in a saucepan and bring it to a temperature of 85°C – just before a full simmer – but do not let it boil. Now pour the warmed milk a little at a time onto the beaten eggs, stirring quite fast with a whisk to prevent the eggs from scrambling.

Pour the egg and milk mix back into the saucepan and cook on a medium heat for 5–7 minutes to thicken it into custard. Keep stirring until the custard coats the back of the spoon. You should get a silky smooth result: if you see any small lumps floating, it means the temperature is too high and you are overcooking the eggs. If this happens, just remove it from the heat and cool.

Once the custard has thickened, remove from the heat and stir in the dark chocolate until it melts. Sieve the cocoa powder into the custard and whisk until combined.

Make sure your smaller bowl is in its ice bath again and pour the custard into it. Whisk while it is cooling to keep it smooth. When it is completely cool, whip your double cream to soft peaks and then fold it into the custard with a metal spoon so you don't lose the air in it.

This is your *base gelato*. Pour it into your ice cream machine and let it do its job for around 30 minutes. Freeze the ice cream until needed or serve immediately.

If you don't have an ice cream machine, don't worry. Put the *base gelato* in the freezer for 6–8 hours. Every 30 minutes or so, take the mix out and give it a good stir with a fork to avoid the formulation of big ice crystals. Smaller ice crystals mean a smoother gelato.

GELATO AL CARAMELLO SALATO (SALTED CARAMEL ICE CREAM)

Lab G   Makes 1 litre

Lab G is famous for its salted caramel gelato. Made to a completely different style of base from most ice creams, it has a soft texture that is pure luxury. Once you've tasted it, you'll understand exactly why people queue up for it.

300g caster sugar

1 teaspoon sea salt

40g salted butter

500ml whole milk

200ml double cream

2 large free range egg yolks

In a deep saucepan with plenty of space, melt the caster sugar on a moderate heat. Using a non-stick, heat-resistant spatula, stir it constantly – let it burn for flavour, you want the sugar to caramelise. It will look like it is forming clumps just before it melts. Don't panic, just keep stirring. When the sugar has melted and is starting to turn a clear dark golden colour, add the salt and allow it to dissolve. Add the butter next. At this point the temperature will be 160°C and the butter will spit and bubble so take care.

Reduce the heat and stir until the butter has melted into the caramel. Bit by bit, pour in the milk and cream. Watch out for it bubbling in case it burns you. Stir steadily with a whisk and cook it for a few minutes until you get a smooth golden sauce.

Put some ice in a large bowl, then put a smaller bowl on the ice, making sure it's quite dry inside, to form an ice bath. In this smaller bowl beat the egg yolks. Gently pour your golden caramel sauce onto the egg yolks and mix very fast with your whisk to prevent the eggs from scrambling. Stir this custard until smooth and then leave it in its ice bath until it is completely cool.

When it's cold, put the custard into your ice cream machine and churn according to the instructions of your model. If you don't have an ice cream machine, freeze it for 8 hours, stirring with a fork every 30 minutes or so to stop ice crystals forming.

Due to the high sugar content of this gelato, you will get a very soft finish after the machine churns it and it will need to set in the freezer for 2–3 hours.

GELATO ALLA STRACCIATELLA (CHOCOLATE CHIP ICE CREAM)

Lab G   Makes 1 litre

The Italians love *stracciatella* ice cream and give it a much more grown-up twist than our 'choc chip' by using dark bitter chocolate. The contrast of the super smooth gelato and the hard chocolate pieces works beautifully and this flavour was always my favourite as a kid.

This method of making gelato is known as a *base bianca*. It has no eggs and relies on heating the milk to thicken it slightly.

1 vanilla pod
450ml whole milk
250g caster sugar
350ml double cream
120g dark chocolate

Cut the vanilla pod in half lengthways, taking out the seeds with the tip of a knife. Then add the pod and the seeds to the milk and the sugar in a saucepan. Gently heat the milk, sugar and vanilla on the stove until it reaches 85°C (or just before it simmers).

Fill a large bowl with ice, place a smaller bowl inside it on the ice to create an ice bath and then pour the hot, sweet milk into the smaller bowl to cool, discarding the vanilla pod. Once it is completely cooled, whip your double cream to soft peaks and fold it into the milk mixture using a metal spoon. This is your base bianca.

Pour the **base bianca** into the ice cream machine and churn for about 30 minutes. If you don't have an ice cream machine, use the freezer method: put the base bianca in the freezer for 6–8 hours. Every 30 minutes or so, take it out and give it a good stir with a fork.

When the gelato is almost finished churning, carefully shave the dark chocolate with a sharp knife and add a bit at a time. If you use the freezer method, add the chocolate when the gelato is thick enough that it doesn't sink to the bottom. Serve the ice cream immediately.

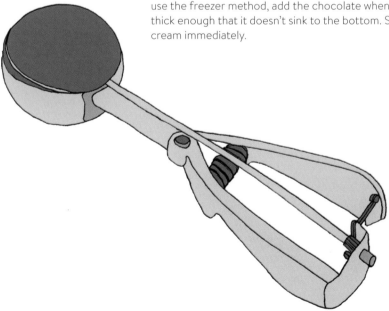

GELATO ALLA FRAGOLA (STRAWBERRY ICE CREAM)

Lab G   Makes 1 litre

....

This ice cream is an Italian take on the classic of strawberries and cream. It tastes like a summer's afternoon, no matter what time of the year you eat it...

1 vanilla pod
450ml whole milk
220g caster sugar
350ml double cream
250g fresh strawberries

This ice cream uses the base bianca. Cut the vanilla pod in half and scrape out the seeds with the tip of a knife. Put the pod and seeds in a pan with the milk and sugar and heat gently until it reaches 85°C (just before it simmers). Fill a large bowl with ice, set a smaller one inside it to create an ice bath and then pour the sweet milk into this smaller bowl to cool. Discard the vanilla pod.

In a food processor, blend your washed, dried and hulled strawberries to a purée and mix into the completely cool milk mixture. Then whip your double cream to soft peaks and fold it into the milk and strawberries with a balloon whisk to keep the air in.

Pour into the ice cream machine and churn for about 30 minutes, or put it into the freezer for 6–8 hours, stirring with a fork every 30 minutes or so.

PUFF PUFF (SPICED FRIED DOUGH BALLS)

Inspired by Iya-Ibadan   Makes 30–35

These little balls of fried dough are made with yeast and lightly spiced. They are popular throughout West Africa and have several different names. Ghanaians call them *togbei* while Nigerians and Cameroonians call them either *chin chin* or *puff puff*. No matter what they are called, everyone loves the taste, especially at parties.

I've added slightly more spice and omitted the egg and milk some recipes use as this makes them very rich. This version is dairy-free and suitable for vegans. I've also added palm wine for extra flavour, but if you prefer not to use alcohol just use more water.

1 sachet fast-rise dried yeast

150ml warm water

200g self-raising flour

50g plain flour

75g caster sugar

1 teaspoon baking powder

pinch of salt

1 teaspoon ground cinnamon

1 teaspoon ground ginger

½ teaspoon nutmeg, grated

3 tablespoons palm wine or vermouth (optional)

2 tablespoons icing sugar (optional)

1 litre vegetable oil for frying

Mix the yeast with 50ml of the warm water and leave the mixture until it starts to foam.

Sift the flours into a large bowl and stir in the sugar, baking powder, salt and spices. Make a well in the middle and pour in the remaining 100ml of warm water, the yeast mixture you've already made and the palm wine or vermouth. Bring it together with your hand to make a dough, adding more water if it seems too stiff. It should be soft enough to knead. Knead for a minute or two until the dough becomes more smooth and elastic. Put it back in the bowl, cover with a cloth and leave in a warm place to rise for at least an hour or until doubled in size. This puffing up is how the **puff puff** get their name.

Heat the oil to 75–80°C or until a pinch of the dough floats when dropped into it. Then, using your thumb and forefinger, pull off walnut-sized pieces of dough and roll them into balls. Carefully drop the dough balls into the hot oil and cook for about 1–2 minutes on both sides, until the outside is golden and the middle is no longer sticky when you put a fork in it. Remove with a slotted spoon and drain them on kitchen roll or a clean tea towel. I sprinkle them with a little bit of icing sugar before serving. They are best served piping hot.

Brixton stockists note: palm wine can be bought from House of Bottles on Coldharbour Lane.

ANZAC BISCUITS

Inspired by Federation   Makes 18

These biscuits were created, the story goes, to support the Australian and New Zealand forces fighting at Gallipoli in 1915. Easy to make, these chewy oat and coconut biscuits kept well enough to be sent from the Antipodes to the Ottoman Empire for a taste of home. They are now made for Anzac Day on 25th April each year to remember the troops.

Given the biscuits are associated worldwide with New Zealand, it's no surprise than when Kiwis Nick and George opened Federation in 2010, they brought them to Brixton. Still available every day, Anzac biscuits are one of Federation's best-sellers as they go particularly well with a good cup of coffee.

125g butter, cubed

2 tablespoons golden syrup

2 tablespoons cold water

100g rolled oats

50g desiccated coconut

125g plain flour

100g soft brown sugar

½ teaspoon bicarbonate of soda

Preheat the oven to 160°C and line three baking trays with greaseproof paper.

Melt the butter and golden syrup in a pan along with the cold water. While these are melting gently, mix the oats, coconut, flour and sugar together in a large bowl and make a well in the middle.

Add the bicarbonate of soda to the melted syrup and butter and stir while it foams. The mixture will thicken and fizz. Pour it in the well in the dry ingredients and stir well until you have a damp, slightly crumbly, oaty dough.

Place the mixture a tablespoon at a time onto the trays and flatten slightly with your hand, making sure you leave room for the biscuits to spread. Bake for 10–12 minutes or until they are golden brown around the edges.

Carefully lift the biscuits onto a wire rack to cool. They will still be quite soft at this stage, but will cool to a lovely chewy crumbly finish that makes it difficult to stop at just one biscuit. If you manage to resist, they will keep for up to a week in a tin.

PEANUT COOKIES

Inspired by Kumasi Market

Peanuts, or groundnuts, are a staple foodstuff in West Africa, providing valuable protein and a satisfying feel to dishes. Usually used in savoury food, they also work as a sweet treat, especially when mixed with brown sugar in these simple, flour-free cookies. The high fat content of the peanut butter acts like dairy butter to make these rich and 'short' in texture, so they melt in the mouth. They rarely last long, especially with kids around.

250g peanut butter or groundnut paste

100g brown sugar

75g shredded coconut or chocolate chips (optional)

1 egg, beaten

1 teaspoon vanilla extract

Put the peanut butter in a large bowl and beat the brown sugar into it until it is well combined and the peanut butter is slightly soft and creamy. Toast the shredded coconut (if you're using it) in a dry frying pan and set it aside.

Add the beaten egg and vanilla to the peanut butter mixture and combine well. If you are using the coconut or chocolate chips, add them now. The dough should come together nicely in the bowl when it's ready. Wrap it in greaseproof paper and chill in the fridge for at least 30 minutes or overnight.

When you're ready to bake the cookies, preheat the oven to 170°C and line two baking trays with greaseproof paper. Take teaspoon-sized balls of the dough and place them on the baking tray, leaving room for them to spread. Then flatten them down slightly with your fingers or the back of a fork.

Bake the cookies for about 12–15 minutes until they seem dry on top and crisped round the edges. Cool on a wire rack. The cookies are quite fragile and crumbly because of the peanut butter, so handle them carefully. Allow them to cool completely and then enjoy.

TRINIDADIAN BANANA BREAD

Fish, Wings & Tings

This bread uses up those ripe bananas you always seem to have left in the bowl and is very simple to make. It goes best with coconut ice cream as a dessert but is also delicious as a snack with a cup of tea.

80g unsalted butter, softened

260g caster sugar

1 large egg

3 very ripe bananas, mashed

1 tablespoon sour cream

1 teaspoon vanilla extract

5 dashes Angostura bitters

1 teaspoon ground cinnamon

180g plain flour

1 teaspoon bicarbonate of soda

1 teaspoon ground nutmeg

¼ teaspoon salt

brown sugar for dusting

2lb/900g loaf tin

Preheat the oven to 180°C and grease and line your loaf tin with greaseproof paper.

Cream together the butter and sugar in a large bowl until lighter in colour and fluffy. Mix in the egg, mashed bananas, sour cream, vanilla, bitters and cinnamon until smooth. Add in the flour, bicarbonate of soda, nutmeg and salt and mix gently until just combined.

Pour the batter into your loaf tin and bake for an hour or until a toothpick inserted into the centre comes out clean. Leave the bread to cool in the tin for 10–15 minutes before turning it out onto a wire rack. Dust the top with the brown sugar while still warm and serve in slices.

CARROT CAKE

Snugg

Serves 8–10

This is the most moist carrot cake you'll ever eat. It uses oil rather than butter which gives it a rich crumb and means the un-iced cake will keep in a tin for up to 6 days. But don't skip the icing when you are ready to eat it: the gorgeous buttercream is enriched with mascarpone to give a slight tang that compliments the sweet cake beautifully.

I like this best as a sandwich cake, but you can also make it as 12 cupcakes or mini loaves– just follow the recipe as below and make half the amount of icing.

For the cake

200ml sunflower or vegetable oil

150g caster sugar

100g soft brown sugar

3 eggs, separated

200g self-raising flour

½ teaspoon ground cloves

½ teaspoon ground cinnamon

½ teaspoon ground ginger

¼ teaspoon cardamom seeds, ground

250g carrots, grated

75g crushed tinned pineapple, drained

1–2 tablespoons pineapple juice (from the tin)

250g desiccated coconut

For the icing

250g icing sugar

250g butter, very soft, cubed

½ teaspoon cardamom seeds, ground

5 drops orange oil (or zest of one small orange)

250–500g mascarpone

handful of pistachios, roughly chopped (optional)

2 x 23cm cake tins

Start by preparing your cake tins. Don't line them with greaseproof paper as it can crisp the base of the cake too much: simply butter and flour the tins thoroughly. Preheat the oven to 165°C.

With an electric hand whisk, beat the oil and the two sugars together well until syrupy. This will take 3–4 minutes. Add the egg yolks one at a time, and beat them into the oil and sugar until the mixture looks even glossier. With the whisk still running, add the flour and spices, then the carrots, crushed pineapple and its juice. Stop as soon as everything is combined. Wash the beaters of the whisk well.

In a clean, grease-free bowl, whisk the egg whites with the clean beaters until they form soft peaks. Fold them into the cake batter with a metal spoon, and then gently fold in the desiccated coconut.

Pour the batter into your greased and floured cake tins and bake for 30–35 minutes. They are ready when a toothpick poked into the centre comes out clean or when the cake bounces back when pressed with your thumb. Turn the cakes out of the tins as soon as possible and allow to cool completely on a wire rack.

While the cake is cooling, make the icing. Sift the icing sugar onto the butter and begin beating it with the electric whisk. As soon as it starts to combine, beat in the cardamom seeds and the orange zest or oil. Add the mascarpone one spoonful at a time. The amount you use depends how creamy you like your icing. Stop beating as soon as the mascarpone is mixed in to prevent the icing separating from over mixing.

Using a palette knife, generously smooth half of the icing onto the top of one of the cakes. Dip the knife into boiling water if the icing starts to drag. Repeat this with the second cake and then carefully place it on top of the first cake so you have a sandwich with the icing on top. Sprinkle with chopped pistachios if you like and serve.

FIG, HONEY AND PISTACHIO CAKE

Snugg

Makes 12 mini loaf cakes or a 2lb loaf cake

This cake works especially well as mini loaves like Snugg serve on their platters. You end up with a sticky sweet crunchy base to the cake that goes beautifully with the soft figgy crumb. It has a lovely Middle Eastern feel and is perfect for those figs you buy that go from ready-to-eat to over-ripe in what seems like a few minutes. Use a good quality, preferably local honey to add an extra dimension of flavour.

175g butter

12 teaspoons honey

150g pistachios, chopped

3 eggs

150g caster sugar

100g soft brown sugar

5 fresh figs, chopped into eighths

150g ground almonds

150g self-raising flour

12 mini loaf tins (or a 2lb loaf tin)

Preheat the oven to 165°C. Melt your butter in a small pan and leave it to cool down but not solidify again. This tip from Ella adds moisture to the cake and stops the almonds from making it heavy.

Grease and flour your loaf tins well. Drizzle a teaspoon of honey into the base of each and then scatter with about a teaspoon of the chopped pistachios. (Put all the honey and nuts into the base of a large loaf tin if using.)

Put the eggs in a large bowl with both sugars and, using an electric hand whisk, beat until they come together in a thick, billowy, custardy texture. This will take 4–5 minutes and adds air instead of using extra raising agents.

Add the chopped figs, including the skins, and keep beating the eggs and sugar together. The figs will break up to further thicken the mixture. Fold the ground almonds in with a metal spoon using a chopping motion to keep the air in. Fold the flour in the same way, bit by bit.

When the flour is fully incorporated, swiftly stir the cooled melted butter and any remaining chopped pistachios into the batter. Use an ice cream scoop to ladle equal amounts of batter into the mini loaf tins, allowing room for the batter to rise, or pour it into a 2lb loaf tin.

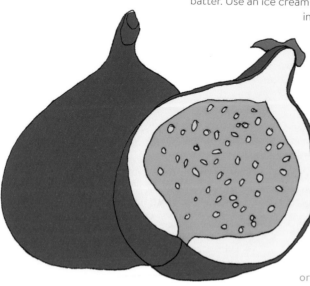

Bake for 25–30 minutes for mini loaf tins or 45 minutes for the larger loaf: the cake is ready when the texture is springy and a toothpick comes out clean. Leave the loaves in the tins for no longer than 5 minutes before turning out onto a wire rack.

Either eat hot to enjoy the soft sticky honey, or allow to cool completely to get the contrast in textures. The cakes will keep for up to 4 days in a tin.

Brixton stockists note: depending on the season you may be able to get local or single flower honey from Cornercopia.

GUINNESS BOILED CAKE

Inspired by Viva Afro Caribbean Food Store   Serves 8

It might not seem like it at first glance, but Ireland and Nigeria have something in common. Both countries love Guinness. Some say the black stuff doesn't taste right unless it's brewed in Dublin, but I'm not sure they've tasted export Guinness brewed in Nigeria. Foreign Extra Stout, to give its full title, packs a stronger and more hoppy flavour at 7.5%. Like alcoholic treacle it makes fruit cake something special.

My granny would never have seen a bottle of the export Guinness in rural Ireland and I'm not sure she'd have approved of the strength of it, but she did know a good cake when she saw one. This is her recipe for boiled cake where the fruit is literally boiled in liquid to make it dark, sticky and moist. Traditional in Northern Ireland, this cake is quick to make but lasts well so you always have some when people drop in.

350g raisins (or mixed dried fruit of your choice)

175g sugar

115g butter

250ml Guinness Foreign Extra Stout

350g plain flour

1¼ teaspoons bicarbonate of soda

1 teaspoon mixed spice

1 egg, beaten

23cm wide, 7cm deep springform cake tin

Put the dried fruit, sugar, butter and Guinness in a saucepan and boil for 20 minutes. This plumps up the fruit and infuses it with flavour.

Grease your cake tin well with butter. Preheat the oven to 180°C.

Sift the flour in a large bowl and add the bicarbonate of soda and mixed spice. Stir in the boiled fruit and any remaining liquid. Add in the beaten egg and stir until just combined. It will come together like a dough rather than a batter. Put into your tin and smooth the top down.

Bake in the oven for 45 minutes. Check the cake at this stage with a skewer. If it comes out slightly sticky, it needs more time. However, I find the dried fruit on top starts to burn slightly at this stage, so I reduce the heat to 170°C and give it another 15 minutes.

Cool the cake on a rack and serve in slices with a strong cuppa. It will keep in a tin for several weeks and actually improves with age as it gets softer and stickier.

LEMBLUCA CAKE

Sponge and Cream

This beautiful cake is rich with lemon and blueberries and happens to be gluten-free because that's the flour that suits it best. Anyone will enjoy it whether they can eat gluten or not. Like all Paulina's cakes, it is simple and luxurious without any window dressing. Perfect to eat on a warm summer's day with homemade lemonade, but made in the winter it will remind you of brighter days!

Doves Farm make both xanthum gum and gluten-free flours, and their products are widely available in wholefood shops and supermarkets.

For the cake:

250g gluten-free plain flour

145g gluten-free self-raising flour

1 tablespoon xanthum gum

1¼ teaspoons gluten-free baking powder

1 teaspoon bicarbonate of soda

½ teaspoon salt

210g unsalted butter

500g caster sugar

125ml lemon juice

zest of ½ a lemon

5 eggs

315ml buttermilk

200g blueberries (reserve 24 for decorating)

For the frosting:

125g unsalted butter, softened

500g icing sugar

225g full-fat cream cheese

zest of 1 lemon

3 x 20cm sandwich tins

Preheat the oven to 180°C. Butter and flour the cake tins and put a circle of greaseproof paper in the base of each.

Mix the two flours, xanthum gum, baking powder, bicarbonate of soda and salt in a large bowl and set aside.

Cream the butter and sugar together until light and fluffy – this is easiest with an electric hand whisk or stand mixer. Add the lemon juice and zest and beat until just combined. The mixture will now look curdled, but don't panic. Beat the eggs in one at a time.

Sift the dry ingredients into the egg and butter mix. Add in the buttermilk and mix it all slowly until just combined. Toss the blueberries in and mix on a higher speed until the batter is smooth and sticky. Some berries will burst and others will remain whole.

Divide the mixture between the three cake tins, smoothing the tops down. Bake for about 25 minutes or until a skewer poked in the middle comes out clean. Allow the cakes to cool in the tins for 10 minutes, and then lift them out and allow to cool completely on a rack.

While they're cooling, make the frosting: make sure the unsalted butter is at room temperature before you start. Put it and the icing sugar in a large bowl and mix slowly until the mixture thickens. Add the cream cheese and continue mixing slowly. Once it is thoroughly combined, mix more quickly until the frosting becomes pale and smooth. Mix in the lemon zest, and then put it in the fridge for 20 minutes to rest.

To assemble the cake, use some of the cooled frosting to sandwich the three layers together. Then apply a very thin layer around the whole cake with a palette knife or spatula. This is the crumbing process and it helps to stick all the crumbs to the sides and top of the cake before you put on the final layer of frosting.

Leave the remaining frosting at room temperature, but put the cake in the fridge to set for 30 minutes. Once the sides and top are firm to touch, apply the frosting to the cake. Once the top and sides are frosted, decorate the top with the reserved blueberries and serve.

Brixton stockists note: you can get Doves Farm products in Brixton Wholefoods.

PEAR AND LAVENDER CAKE

Snugg

Serves 8–10

This a wonderful cake with an unusual flavour combination, just as at home at an English picnic as an autumnal harvest table. It is a show-stopping cake thanks to the layer of caramelised pears under the sweet cream filling, and a subtle drizzle of lavender sugar syrup. You'll have some of the syrup left over and it works beautifully in a Martini, meaning that when I make this cake, I get to combine two of my favourite things...

For the sugar syrup:

120g caster sugar

1 teaspoon dried lavender

120ml water

For the cake:

4 pears (about 240g in total)

1 teaspoon dried lavender

250g caster sugar

200ml vegetable or sunflower oil

3 eggs, separated

250g self-raising flour

For the filling:

250ml double cream

1 heaped tablespoon caster sugar

2 x 23cm cake tins

Preheat the oven to 175°C. Grease your cake tins with butter and flour them lightly.

Make the syrup by heating the sugar and a teaspoon of dried lavender in the water in a small pan until the sugar melts and the syrup is thick and glossy and coats the back of a spoon. Strain to remove the lavender.

For the cake, peel and slice one of the pears thinly, and fan the slices round the base of one of the cake tins. Leave the other tin plain. Brush the fragrant syrup over the sliced pear, building up several layers, and over the floured base of the second tin.

In a large bowl, add another teaspoon of lavender to the caster sugar and then beat it with the oil until you have a thick syrup. It is best to use an electric hand whisk to do this. Add the egg yolks one at a time and beat until they're thoroughly combined and the mixture looks glossier. Beat in the flour. The mixture may look slightly stiff and biscuit-like at this stage – don't worry.

Peel and grate the remaining pears and add them and any liquid that comes off them to the cake mixture: it will start to look like a batter at this stage. Don't be tempted to add any extra pear if it doesn't look wet enough because your pears aren't very ripe. They will release liquid when they cook. Wash the beaters of the electric whisk well.

Whisk the egg whites in a clean, grease-free bowl until they form soft peaks. Fold them into the cake batter with a metal spoon to keep the air in. Pour the batter into your prepared cake tins and bake for 30–35 minutes. They are ready when a toothpick poked into the centre comes out clean or when the cake bounces back when pressed with your thumb. Don't go by colour alone as they turn a darker caramelised colour than a regular sponge because of the pears.

Turn the cakes out of the tins onto a wire rack within 5 minutes of removing them from the oven – otherwise the sugar syrup will make them stick as it cools. The cakes are quite fragile and may crack slightly: hold your nerve, handle them carefully and stick any rogue pear slices back on while no one is looking. Allow the cakes to cool completely.

Whip the cream and the sugar for the filling until the cream forms soft peaks. Put the cake with the caramelised pears on your serving plate with the pear side up and spread the cream over the pears using a palette knife. Gently put the other cake on top to form a sandwich and serve.

You can also make the cake in mini loaf tins. Put one slice of pear in the bottom of each tin and brush the tops of the cakes with the lavender syrup while they are cooling.

Brixton stockists note: buy the dried lavender by weight in Brixton Wholefoods on Atlantic Road.

DRINKS

BRIXTON VILLAGE CHAI TEA

Snugg

Instead of using a pre-blended chai teabag with a muted taste, follow this recipe for a strong and flavoursome version, packed with fresh rich aromas. The mix of spices will rejuvenate you at any time of the day. Use loose leaf tea, preferably a rich malty Assam or rose-infused blend for a soft floral hint.

To serve more than one, scale the tea, water, milk and rosewater up as needed.

1 heaped teaspoon loose leaf tea

1 cup boiling water

2 whole cloves

4 coriander seeds

2 bay leaves

4 grates of a whole nutmeg

2 pods green cardamom

2.5cm cinnamon stick or bark

2 teaspoons condensed milk

½ teaspoon rosewater
(if using Assam)

milk to your preference

Put your loose leaf tea in a pan and add the boiling water. Add the cloves, coriander, bay, nutmeg, cardamom and cinnamon and bring to the boil. Add the condensed milk and bring back to the boil, stirring well to combine. Add fresh milk to taste and boil again briefly. Strain it through a tea strainer or sieve into a cup. Add the rosewater if using and serve.

Brixton stockists note: you can buy rosewater in the Faiz Food Store on 1st Avenue or the Nour Cash & Carry in neighbouring Market Row. You can buy all the spices there too for ease.

BRIXTON HOT CHOCOLATE

Snugg   Serves 1

This is the richest and most decadent hot chocolate around. It will warm you up on even the coldest night. Flavour it with chilli flakes to really warm your cockles or try ground ginger, cinnamon or cardamom. Don't be alarmed by the butter: it gives it a real smoothness.

1 cup whole milk

1 heaped teaspoon dark chocolate drops or chunks

1 teaspoon boiling water

2 teaspoons condensed milk

pinch of chilli flakes, ground ginger, cinnamon or cardamom

small knob butter

Heat the milk in a pan, watching carefully so it doesn't boil over. Put the chocolate in your cup and add the boiling water. Stir the chocolate until it melts. Add the condensed milk to the warm milk in the pan and heat through, stirring well to combine. Pour the hot milk onto the chocolate and stir thoroughly to make sure it's completely melted. Flavour with your choice of spice and put the knob of butter on top to melt. Serve immediately.

HOT BUTTERED RUM

Snugg

It is no secret that Brixton Village gets chilly. In the winter months, the restaurants have fleece blankets outside and people wrap up in them while they eat. The perfect antidote for the chill is hot buttered rum. It is inspired by Cindy from accessories boutique United 80 who, along with her partner Chris, provides the music at Snugg at the weekends. Cindy is well-versed in the cold in the market as her mum had a unit there when she was a kid and, of course, she's a current trader herself.

Don't just take her word for it; make yourself one today. Much more stylish than thermals...

1 teaspoon unsalted butter, softened

1 teaspoon maple syrup

½ teaspoon ground allspice

juice of ½ a lime

50ml golden rum

cinnamon stick, to garnish

freshly grated nutmeg, to garnish

Mix the softened butter, syrup and allspice together to make a thick and creamy whipped butter. Put it in the bottom of a heatproof coffee glass or mug.

Fill the glass up about two thirds with boiling water and mix with a spoon until the butter has melted and emulsified in the liquid, like mixing a salad dressing. Squeeze the lime juice in and stir again; then add the rum.

Using a lighter or a gas flame, lightly warm the cinnamon stick, taking care not to burn it. Add it to the hot rum as a stirrer and then garnish the glass with freshly grated nutmeg.

Brixton stockists note: you need to use a good quality rum for this. Something smooth like Bacardi 8 or Mount Gay Eclipse would be perfect. Ask Tony in House of Bottles for his recommendation.

FRESH GINGER BEER

Fish, Wings & Tings

Makes 2½ litres

This is spicy and refreshing at any time of the day. Unlike the ginger beer the Famous Five drank, it doesn't ferment so is great for kids. Adults can also add a hearty slug of dark rum to make it that much more grown up...

500g fresh ginger
2½ litres cold water
1kg caster sugar

Peel the fresh ginger: the quickest way is to use the edge of a teaspoon. Grate by hand or in a food processor. Bring the water to the boil in a large pot and add the ginger and sugar. Remove from the heat once the sugar has dissolved and steep overnight.

Strain the mixture through a fine sieve or muslin cloth, squeezing out every last bit of liquid. Bottle the ginger beer, making sure you don't screw the caps too tight in case it expands slightly. Refrigerate and drink chilled. It is best drunk within 24 hours.

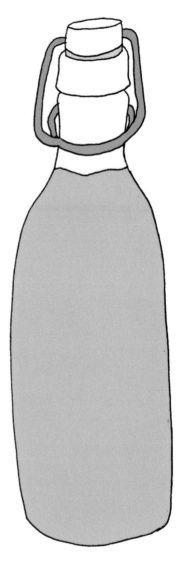

SORREL DRINK

Etta's Seafood Kitchen

Makes 2½ litres

Sorrel drink is made from dried hibiscus flowers, and this cleansing sweet and sour beverage is so associated with Jamaica that the Mexicans call hibiscus *flor de Jamaica*. Sorrel is traditional at Christmas time in Jamaica. It can also have rum in it if you prefer to give it a little kick...

2½ litres cold water

1 packet of hibiscus flowers (about 250g)

500g sugar, plus more if required

4 whole cloves

5cm fresh ginger, peeled and grated

Put the water in a large pot and bring to a boil on the stove — the water must be boiling when you add the hibiscus flowers. Scatter in the flowers and take the pot off the heat immediately. Stir in the sugar, cloves and grated ginger until the sugar is dissolved, and leave to cool overnight. The flowers will steep and infuse to give a rounded flavour.

Strain the drink through a muslin cloth to remove the flowers and spices, and check the sweetness. If you like it less tart, make a quick sugar syrup by heating equal parts sugar to water until the sugar has dissolved, and add to taste.

You can drink the sorrel immediately or it can be bottled and stored in the fridge until needed.

Brixton stockists note: in the autumn and around Christmas time, you will get fresh sorrel flowers at Esme's Organic Grocers in Market Row. Incredibly beautiful as well as flavoursome, they are a real treat. The rest of the year, you can get dried hibiscus from the Nour Cash & Carry.

GUINNESS PUNCH

Inspired by Viva Afro-Caribbean Food Store

Despite being Irish I never drank Guinness until I moved to Lambeth and was introduced to Guinness Punch. Sweet and creamy and incredibly easy to drink, this traditional Caribbean beverage mixes stout, condensed milk and Nurishment over ice for a long refreshing drink that does, in fact, pack quite a punch. It is known in Jamaica as a 'strong back' drink and some suggest it increases men's virility.

Because I don't have a particularly sweet tooth, I stop this from being cloying by using the famous Foreign Extra Stout which is Guinness brewed in Nigeria. At 7.5%, it's much stronger than regular Guinness and has a distinctive hoppy taste that is more bitter than the Irish version. It works beautifully here and you'll find the punch goes down easily on a hot day. It is traditionally served after lunch on a Sunday and would precede a nap very nicely....

100g oats

250ml water

2 x 330ml bottles of Guinness Foreign Extra Stout

1 x 397g can condensed milk

1 x 400g can vanilla flavour Nurishment (or whole milk)

1 teaspoon vanilla extract

5 drops Angostura bitters

½ teaspoon fresh nutmeg, grated

ice to serve

In a large bowl, soak the oats for at least an hour or overnight in the water. Blend the oats and soaking liquid to make a thick oat milk. While the oats are soaking, chill the Guinness, condensed milk and Nurishment.

Pour the oat milk, Guinness, condensed milk and Nurishment together in a large jug or punch bowl and mix well. Add the vanilla extract and the bitters and then sprinkle the nutmeg on top. Serve in glasses, over ice (but don't add the ice to the jug or punch bowl as it will dilute the creaminess). You can also add a tot of rum to the punch if you like.

Brixton stockists note: you can buy the Guinness at the House of Bottles on Coldharbour Lane. Nurishment is available anywhere in Brixton.

ELDERFLOWER CORDIAL

Cornercopia

At Cornercopia, they like to use the natural bounty of the world around them and keep old traditions alive through things like preserves and cordials. Here is one of their favourites.

Elderflower cordial is delicious with sparkling water and a slice of lemon – it also goes very well indeed with sparkling wine or as the base for a summer cocktail. Mix with English white wine, cucumber and strawberries for an English sangria. You will find elderflowers growing in urban gardens, city parks, hedgerows, woods or even wasteland. It often grows where nothing else survives and it's a sign for me that summer is on its way when the fragrant flowers open.

20 elderflower heads

1.5kg caster sugar

1.2 litres cold water

75g citric acid powder

2 lemons, cut into slices

Cut large clusters of flowers from an elderflower tree, making sure you avoid trees close to main roads. Make sure the flowers are dry when you pick them and shake them to rid them of any insects. Remove the flowers from the stalks (which make the cordial bitter) and put them in a large bowl.

Put the sugar and the cold water in a large pan and bring to the boil to make a syrup. Remove the pan from the heat and leave to cool. Pour the syrup over the flowers and mix in the citric acid and lemon slices. Leave overnight to steep.

Next day strain the syrup through a clean muslin cloth into a large bowl or pan to remove the flowers and lemon slices. Pour into clean glass or plastic bottles and store in the fridge: it will keep for several months.

You can save the lemon slices and freeze them in a single layer on silicone paper; then add to your summer drinks for extra flavour.

Brixton stockists note: you can't buy elderflowers commercially but you can forage for them in Wyck Gardens or Brockwell Park, both of which are in Brixton but far enough from a main road to be good for foraging. You can buy citric acid in the Nour Cash & Carry or any pharmacy.

FLY AWAY HOME

The Botanical at Cornercopia   Serves 1

This cocktail was served at Cornercopia's cocktail pop-up, The Botanical, over summer 2013 and was created by Nicholas Horton. It is a twist on the classic Aviation, which involves gin, lemon and violet liqueur. This 'goose'-berry version takes its name from the eponymous film where the main characters follow the migrating trajectory of wild geese on a small plane. Before you make the cocktail, you need to make gooseberry-infused gin and sour some fresh ginger beer.

Ossie's Fresh Ginger is an institution in Brixton. Ossie makes it locally from a West African recipe using fresh root ginger, and here it is soured and used instead of lemon juice. If you can't get your hands on Ossie's, try Fish, Wings & Tings' ginger beer on page 165 instead.

For the gooseberry-infused gin:

10 gooseberries

300ml classic style gin, such as Sipsmith

Cut the gooseberries in half and freeze until solid. Once frozen, put them in a 350ml capacity jar, and then top it up with the gin: as the gooseberries thaw in the gin, they will release even more flavour. Leave for a couple of days to infuse.

For the soured ginger:

1 tablespoon citric acid powder

250ml Ossie's Fresh Ginger

Stir the citric acid into the Fresh Ginger and stir until dissolved. It should then have a pH of 2.3 (the same acidity level as lemon juice) which sours the ginger beer for the cocktail.

For the cocktail:

50ml gooseberry-infused gin

25ml soured Ossie's Fresh Ginger

1 egg white

15ml elderflower cordial (see page 168)

15ml violet liqueur

large handful of ice cubes

Put all the ingredients into a shaker and dry shake, with no ice. This will emulsify the egg. Add the ice, shake again and double strain through a mesh strainer in order to avoid any unpleasant little shards of ice. Serve in a chilled coupette.

Brixton stockists note: you can buy Ossie's Fresh Ginger Beer in Cornercopia.

MS B'S LONG ISLAND ICED TEA

Snugg   Serves 1

This is the perfect cocktail to get the night started in Brixton Village. You'll certainly find your dancing feet after a few...

100ml cola

25ml gin

25ml vodka

25ml white rum

dash Cointreau

1 slice of orange, juiced

3 limes, juiced

1 drop orange blossom water

orange zest to serve

Fill a tall glass two thirds full with ice cubes. Pour the cola over the ice and allow it to chill for a minute or two.

Add about 5 ice cubes to a cocktail shaker and add the gin, vodka and rum, along with the dash of Cointreau. Squeeze the juice from the slice of orange and the limes in as well. Include the skins of the fruit. Finish with the drop of orange blossom water and shake well.

Strain the liquid out onto the cola and dress with orange zest and a stirrer. I added a cocktail umbrella too. Your capacity for kitsch may vary.

Brixton stockists note: the orange blossom water is available in the Nour Cash & Carry in neighbouring Market Row.

PEA BRUME

The Botanical at Cornercopia

Serves 1

Always at the forefront in the Village and keeping things fresh, Cornercopia hosted a cocktail pop-up over summer 2013. Their dining room featured a custom-built bar and became The Botanical. Run by up-and-coming cocktail king Nicholas Horton, it featured homemade cordials and bitters using seasonal and foraged ingredients, and each drink had that Cornercopia twist.

You may never have thought to make a cocktail with fresh peas before, but you'll be amazed how well it works. Nicholas created this specially to capture the sweet flavours of summer peas and its originality stood out. But it was its smooth flavour that made it so popular.

The name of the cocktail evokes spring time – fresh and delicate fogs – which Nick thought suited the cocktail to perfection, playing as it does on the idea of the London 'pea-souper' fogs of the 50s. It is to be pronounced with a slight rolling 'r'.

For the spearmint syrup:

15g fresh spearmint leaves

500g caster sugar

250ml cold water

Blanch the mint leaves in plenty of boiling water for 45 seconds and then plunge them into iced water to stop them cooking. Put them in a pan with the sugar and 250ml of water, and heat gently until the sugar dissolves. Once the syrup is thick and glossy, remove it from the heat and cool in an ice bath. Bottle when cold: it will keep in the fridge for several weeks.

For the cocktail

100g fresh, shelled peas

50ml Bermondsey gin

10ml spearmint syrup

3 drops wormwood bitters

Freeze the peas, and then soak them in hot water before passing through a microjuicer. Alternatively, blend them with a small amount of water and then squeeze the purée through a cheesecloth or muslin. Put 25ml of the pea juice into a cocktail shaker with the rest of the ingredients and some ice. Shake well and double strain through a mesh strainer into a chilled coupette. Enjoy!

RHUBARB GIN FIZZ

The Botanical at Cornercopia   Serves 1

This is Nicholas Horton's signature drink and uses Boxer gin which is intensely citrus and has a strong juniper flavour. If you can't get it use another premium gin, preferably export strength. This cocktail also uses a saffron syrup and a vanilla shrub – or syrup made with vinegar instead of water. It's absolutely worth the effort to make these: the saffron lends a beautiful colour and subtle flavour to the drink, and the vanilla shrub has the effect of both sweetening the rhubarb and enhancing its natural acidity. Don't omit them.

For the saffron syrup:

250g caster sugar

pinch of saffron

125ml water

Put the sugar and saffron in a pan with the water and heat until the sugar has dissolved. Once the syrup becomes thick and glossy, remove it from the heat and cool in an ice bath. Bottle when cold – it will keep in the fridge for several weeks.

For the vanilla shrub:

250ml white wine vinegar

125g caster sugar

1 vanilla pod

Put all the ingredients in a saucepan and simmer at the lowest possible heat until all the sugar has melted. Remove from the heat and cool in an ice bath. When the shrub is quite cold, strain out the vanilla pod and bottle. It will keep in the fridge for several weeks.

For the cocktail:

1–2 rhubarb stalks

50ml Boxer gin

25ml egg white (about 1 small egg white)

15ml saffron syrup

15ml vanilla shrub

handful of ice cubes

Juice the rhubarb stalks and pour a 25ml measure of the juice into a cocktail shaker. Add the rest of the ingredients and dry shake (without ice) to properly emulsify the egg white. Then add ice and shake again.

Double strain the cocktail through mesh into a chilled coupette. Garnish with candied dried rhubarb skin or a small stalk of fresh rhubarb. Enjoy!

Brixton stockists note: Boxer gin is sold in Cornercopia in refillable bottles. If you can't get it, use another smooth, premium, export strength gin.

TAMARIND MARGARITA

Jalisco   Serves 1

Wilson is on a mission to bring good margaritas to Brixton. Too often tequila in this country is seen as something to be forced down, disguised with salt and lemon, but mixed well it is to be savoured and enjoyed. Combined here with the tang of tamarind, these margaritas are very moreish and easy to make. They will change your mind on tequila!

Use tamarind pulp for the best flavour here. Wilson also uses silver tequila which is tequila that has been distilled twice and is smoother and cleaner to drink.

For the tamarind syrup:

40g tamarind pulp

100g sugar

500ml water

Break up the tamarind pulp and put it in a pan with the sugar and the water. Heat gently for 30 minutes and then strain it all though a sieve, pushing the pulp with a spoon. Retain the dark syrup and throw the debris in the sieve away. Chill the syrup until needed. It will keep for several weeks.

For the margarita:

50ml tamarind syrup

1 tablespoon granulated sugar

35ml tequila

20ml Triple Sec

Before you shake the margarita, pour a small amount of the tamarind syrup on a saucer. Pour some granulated sugar onto another saucer. Dip the rim of your glass into the saucer of syrup and then into the sugar.

Fill a cocktail shaker with ice and pour the tequila, Triple Sec and tamarind syrup over it. Shake well to mix and chill, and strain.

Serve in the sugar-rimmed glass over plenty of ice.

GLOSSARY OF TERMS

This glossary covers both ingredients and items you can buy in the market from specific traders. It also translates the wide difference in terms for the same ingredients used across the world and around Brixton Village itself. Both the traders and I were less confused when we discovered we all had different names for the same things!

Achiote: also known as annatto, this seed is used throughout South America, the Caribbean and the Philippines to add flavour and colour to food. Tasting a bit like nutmeg, it can be used in place of turmeric or saffron.

Ackee: this tree fruit from Jamaica is most closely associated with the national dish ackee and saltfish. A bright red bell-shaped fruit, the flesh of the raw ackee is cream with large glossy black seeds. These must be discarded as they are poisonous. Ackee is yellow when cooked and looks similar to scrambled egg. It has a delicate flavour and is available in tins in the UK.

African land snails: these are the largest land snail in the world. It is not uncommon for one to grow to be 20cm long. Kept as pets in the West for their sedate nature, they are seen as one of the world's most invasive species in their native area of West Africa. They can destroy crops and livelihoods, and can create up to 1000 offspring each per year. They are often captured and used for food in this region. Regarded as a delicacy, they are fed a special diet to clean them out, and then de-shelled and cleaned with alum before cooking.

Alligator pepper: this spice is related to the ginger family and named for the pod it comes in which has bumps similar to an alligator's back. It is also known as 'grains of paradise', *mbongo spice* and *melegueta*. It has a lemony, peppery flavour with a hint of black cardamom. Use as you would peppercorns or cardamom. It is highly prized in West Africa.

All purpose seasoning: this is used widely in Caribbean cooking to flavour food. You can make your own using equal amounts of salt, pepper, chilli flakes, nutmeg, garlic powder, annatto, allspice, celery seed and paprika. It will store well when mixed.

Allspice: sometimes known as 'pimento berries' or 'Jamaican pepper'. Allspice is essential in Jamaican cooking, especially in jerk dishes where the berries infuse the marinade and the wood is used to cook the food. It is so named because it seems to combine the taste of cinnamon bark, nutmeg and cloves. It can also be used in sweet dishes that would use these spices.

Alum: used for cleaning African land snails for cooking, it is usually sold as blocks. Its full name is potassium aluminium sulfate. This is the same chemical that gives baking powder its distinct flavour and is perfectly safe for food use.

Amalfi lemons: these fragrant lemons hail from the south of Italy and are regarded as the finest lemons in the world. Larger than the lemons we see here, they are intensely flavoured and usually come with the leaves still attached. The liqueur limoncello is made from them.

Angostura bitters: the best known version of bitters. They, and other bitters, are made of herbs and spices infused in at least 44% alcohol. Used to add flavour to drinks, they are also fantastic in marinades and baking. They are named for the town Angostura in Venezuela rather than involving angostura bark from the tree of the same name.

Annatto: see *achiote*.

Aonori: the Japanese name for 'green seaweed' or 'laver'. It is served on top of *okonomiyaki*.

Arepas: a kind of pancake or flatbread made from corn dough which is particularly popular in Colombia. Eaten as a snack or starter, they are often served with toppings such as cheese or as a filled sandwich, particularly for breakfast.

Bammy: a traditional Jamaican flatbread made from cassava. The small patties are soaked and fried.

Bandeja paisa: the Colombian national dish, this is a platter from Paisa province. Famed for the amount of food, it features beans cooked with salt pork, rice, *arepas*, plantain, chorizo Colombiano, avocado, pork, beef steak and *chicharrón* (fried pork skin).

Bitterleaf: related to chicory, the leaves add a bitterness to Nigerian soups such as *egusi*. Sold fresh or dried, it also has healing properties.

Bodi: this is the Trinidadian name for snake beans or yardlong beans, a climbing vine that produces very long (although not actually a whole yard) green beans. They are commonly eaten as a side dish through the

Caribbean and Asia.

Bonito: a type of non-endangered tuna fish. It is a staple in Japanese cuisine. It is fermented, dried and flaked before being used like fish sauce or Worcestershire sauce to add a savoury flavour to dishes as a garnish or a condiment. The flakes are known as **katsuo bushi**.

Bottom-of-the-pot: this is how Nigerians describe the crust that forms at the bottom of a pot of jollof rice as it cooks. The Spanish call it **socarrat** when they make paella and the Persians call it **tahdig** when they cook rice. It is fought over as the best bit of the whole dish.

Breadfruit: this is a large fruit with dimpled green skin and white flesh, and a bread-like texture. Seen halved on greengrocers stalls, breadfruit can be bought by the size of piece you need – you can also get it in tins. It is delicious fried, but also can be used in sweet dishes or made into gluten-free flour.

Bresaola: this is raw beef that has been salted, spiced and then air dried for several months until dark in colour and slightly chewy. It is usually served in thin slices, but it can also be used to cook with in thicker pieces which are heated through.

Buckwheat: slightly confusingly named, buckwheat not a kind of wheat at all. It is the seed of a flowering plant from the knotweed or Polygonaceae family. Naturally gluten-free, it is eaten as seeds, groats and flour and is particularly popular in Europe. The French use the flour for its nutty flavour in crêpes known as 'galettes'.

Buttermilk: this is the low-fat liquid left over from traditional butter churning when the butter fat separates off. It is often made nowadays by culturing milk with lactic acid bacteria. It is smooth, creamy and tangy in taste. It tenderises meat, helps rise unleavened breads and can be used in cooking instead of yoghurt as it doesn't curdle.

Calabaza pumpkin: a large green-skinned pumpkin, this is also known as 'Jamaican pumpkin'. Usually sold by the slice in the market rather than whole, the skin is thin enough to leave on when cooking. It has a soft texture when cooked that helps thicken dishes slightly.

Callaloo: it is both the Jamaican and Guyanese name for amaranth leaves and the name of a cooked dish made with seafood, salt pork, coconut milk and the leaves of the amaranth or **taro** plants. This dish is derived from a West African speciality called **palava**, which is similar to **callaloo** but also contains okra. **Callaloo** is often thought of as the national dish of Trinidad.

Caraili: the Trinidadian name for a long green knobbly fruit, commonly known as 'bitter melon', or **karela** in Asia or **cerassie** or **corilla** in Jamaica. It is often used in teas to aid digestion or can be eaten in dishes or sauces where its bitter flavour adds depth.

Cassava: a starchy root known as **manioc** in Brazil, **yuca** in Colombia and 'tapioca' in India. It is eaten as a root vegetable, ground into flour known as **fufu** or dried into pearls which are eaten in milk puddings in the UK or fermented into **gari** in Ghana. It is an extremely versatile ingredient, but can be difficult to digest in large quantities.

Chadon beni: also known as **culantro** or 'Thai parsley', this herb has a peppery, stronger and slightly more medicinal flavour than the better known cilantro or coriander. A beautiful-looking plant, it has blades rather than leaves. It is especially prized in Trinidadian cooking.

Cho cho: these edible gourds look like a bright green thin-skinned squash with a deep wrinkle in the base. They are known as **christophene** in Trinidad, **chayote** in Central and South America and **mirliton** in Creole and Cajun cooking. **Cho cho** is the Jamaican name for them. They are used in a similar fashion to summer squash or round courgettes. They have a crisp texture and light taste that absorbs flavours well.

Chicharrón: similar to pork scratchings in Britain, these are pork rinds or skin that have been deep-fried. They are popular throughout South America, the Philippines and Spain and are eaten as a snack and as a topping on meals. They are especially popular in Colombia where they form part of the national dish.

Chorizo Colombiano: very different in style to the Spanish paprika-rich cured salami, chorizo in Colombia refers to a coarse ground pork sausage. It is flavoured with garlic, oregano and spring onions and cooked like a traditional British banger. Often longer in length like a frankfurter, they are usually served sliced after cooking.

Christophene: see **cho cho**.

Chunkay: this is a Trinidadian word meaning 'to sauté'.

Clamato: a drink made from tomato juice and clam extract, its savoury flavour is popular in North America and Mexico. Often served with beer to make a *michelada*, it is both satisfying and refreshing.

Cocoyam: this is how the *taro* plant is known in Nigeria, Ghana and parts of Cameroon where the root and leaves are used in soups and stews. Caribbean communities use it in a similar way but call it *dasheen* or *eddo*. Trinidadian people call it *coco*.

Codfish: the Trinidadian term for 'salt cod' or 'saltfish'.

Coriander root: just as it sounds, this is the root of the coriander or cilantro plant. Robust enough for slow cooking compared to the plant's leaves or stalks, coriander can be bought in bunches with the roots attached or you can simply pull them up from a living plant.

Coupette: the style of wide-rimmed glass associated with margaritas and daiquiris.

Crayfish: West African food uses both dried and ground crayfish to add a savoury umami note to soups or stews. These tiny shellfish melt in the stock and are much smaller than the small lobster-like crayfish of Europe and America, with a deeper flavour.

Creole: in culinary terms, Creole food is that which can be traced to the slaves of West Africa when they were brought to the Caribbean, American South and countries such as Brazil. The slave trade not only brought new foods to these regions, but they showed how to cook them too. Over the centuries, ingredients and dishes have adapted and developed from the original West African influence. Creole food is most associated with Louisiana, but is prevalent in the French Caribbean and Portuguese South America too.

Daikon: a large white pointed radish with a peppery flavour. Also known as *mooli*.

Dasheen: another name for the starchy tuber known as *taro* or *cocoyam*. The leaves are known as *dasheen bush* in the Caribbean and used in a similar fashion to spinach.

Dashi konbu: Japanese stock or soup base made from dried bonito tuna with *konbu* seaweed (a type of dried dulse). Simmered to create a rich savoury stock, this can also be bought as *dashi no moto* or instant *dashi*.

Dodo: not a large extinct bird but the common term in Nigeria for fried sliced plantain.

Donabe: a Japanese earthenware pot used for cooking over an open flame or in an oven. Similar in style to a Moroccan tagine.

Eba: a thick dough made from a type of dried, fermented cassava flour called gari. It is served dipped into soups and stews in West Africa.

Eddoes: these are simply the smaller version of the starchy tuber known as *taro* or *dasheen*. They look like a hairy potato with a striped peel which you remove before eating. They have a nutty flavour and can be boiled or fried or mashed. They are an essential ingredient in many Caribbean soups.

Egusi: *egusi* seeds are a type of melon seed. Rich in healthy fatty acids and protein, they are ground and used to thicken *egusi* soup. Particularly popular in Nigeria, this soup contains meat, dried and smoked fish, okra and tomatoes and is served with *eba*.

Ehuru: also known as *calabash* or 'African nutmeg', this is not quite the same botanically as the nutmeg used worldwide. The flavour is similar but less intense, so it is best to roast the spice first.

Flank: sold either as thin steaks or a joint of meat, this cut of beef comes from the back of the abdomen. It is marbled with fat and is excellent in burgers or slow-cooked in South American dishes. You could substitute skirt steak if you can't get flank.

Farro: often confused with spelt or barley, this grain is in fact a strain of wheat known as 'emmer'. Not gluten-free, it has a nutty, chewy texture that is particularly good in soups and salads. It is very popular in Italy, forming the basis of several classic Tuscan dishes.

Galangal: a rhizome often confused with ginger, this is a crucial ingredient in Thai cooking. Smoother skinned than ginger, with attractive pink rings, it is less sweet and more peppery and can be peeled and cooked in the same fashion. It can also be bought dried or powdered, but its unique taste cannot be substituted with anything else.

Garden egg: a small white aubergine which looks like a peeled hard boiled egg (hence the American name of 'eggplant'). It can also be speckled with green. Both kinds are quite bitter compared to purple aubergines.

Gari: a staple foodstuff particularly in Ghana, this is a flour made from grated, soaked and fermented cassava that is then dried to preserve it. *Gari* is used to thicken soups or made into eba.

Gizzards: the secondary stomachs of birds which are used to grind the grain they eat. Pure muscle, they are delicious slow cooked.

Golden Ray margarine: used in Trinidad for cooking, this margarine is coloured a deep yellow colour by annatto. It also adds a unique flavour that is associated with Trini food. You can substitute butter and a drizzle of annatto oil.

Groundnuts: 'peanuts' in the US and UK, they are called 'groundnuts' in West Africa. Actually a legume and member of the bean family, they can be used in sweet and savoury dishes. Groundnut paste is like a smoother, creamier version of peanut butter because it is ground more intensely, so the oils are more emulsified.

Ground provisions: a mixture of starchy vegetables and tubers such as yam, sweet potato, *eddoes*, *dasheen*, *taro*, cassava, breadfruit, plantain, and green bananas (also known as green fig). Boiled and served as a side dish, it is referred to as 'ground provisions' throughout the Caribbean, except Jamaica where it is known as 'hard food'.

Guanabana: also known as *soursop* or *cherimoya*, this dimpled green fruit makes a creamy drink with a hint of tropical flavours. It is especially popular in Colombia.

Guiso: a seasoning of tomatoes and spices for South American beans, it adds flavour in the same way as a *tarka* does to *daal* in Indian food.

Gungo peas: also known as 'pigeon peas', these legumes are often used in Jamaican rice and peas, giving the dish its name and confusing some people who were expecting garden peas instead.

Hominy: kernels of corn that have been dried and treated with lime or other alkalis like lye as a preservative. The kernels are then cooked like any dried pulses. Hominy can also be ground into flour to make corn porridges such as American grits. It is popular through North and South America.

Injera: a large spongy pancake with a distinctive sour flavour, made from fermented teff flour. It is eaten in Eritrea and Ethiopia. Stews are placed directly onto it and the injera is torn off into pieces and used to eat the stew with, like a utensil and side dish in one.

I-tal: deriving from the word 'vital' it describes the unprocessed, very natural and spiritually attuned style of eating that is crucial to the religious beliefs of Rastafarians. Often vegetarian or vegan, ital food never uses pork and Rastafarians abstain from alcohol. Ital food is about increasing feelings of vitality and life, but there are few set rules: for some it means avoiding salted or canned foods, while others eat some fish.

Jackfish: a large blue-tinged fish from the jack or carangidae family, It is found in warm waters especially round the Caribbean. It works well cooked in a stew or pie as the flesh is quite meaty.

Jerk: this name describes both a seasoning and a method of cooking, particularly associated with Jamaica. It is most commonly associated with chicken, but is used with pork and fish as well. The food is marinaded in a jerk seasoning made from allspice, thyme and scotch bonnet peppers. It is then cooked in a jerk drum (a lidded barbecue made from an oil drum) over charcoal made from the wood of the allspice tree for a unique smoky flavour.

June plums: small waxy skinned fruit which are especially popular in the Caribbean. Jamaicans juice them or make preserves while Trinidadians often curry them. Green-skinned when unripe, they become yellow as they ripen which gives them their other name of 'golden apples'. They have a sweet and sour flavour.

Kaffir limes: these are squat wrinkled little limes, essential to Thai cooking. Every part, including the leaves, is used. The flavour and aroma is unlike anything else. The leaves are now quite easy to find outside Thailand and can be dried or frozen until needed. You can sometimes get the dried rind at Chinese supermarkets – it will be labelled *pima grood*. The plants grow well in most climates, allowing you to use the rind and juice more easily.

Kewpie mayonnaise: this brand is so famous it is also known as 'Japanese mayonnaise'. Rich with egg yolks and cider vinegar, it comes in squeezy pouches and is used to top *okonamiyaki*.

Labneh: a soft cheese made from natural yoghurt, *labneh* is made by straining the watery whey out of full-fat yoghurt. Commonly eaten in the Middle East, it is used to top flatbreads or on dishes to cool the heat from chilli.

Larb gai: a very spicy Thai salad made with ground meat, lime juice and chillies.

Lemongrass: a fibrous grass with a beautiful lemony fragrance and flavour, this is mainly used in savoury dishes particularly in Thailand and Vietnam. It is used to infuse food, but is rarely eaten due to its texture.

Liquid Smoke: very popular in Colombia, this is the essence of wood smoke in a bottle. It adds an outdoor feel to any dish.

Locust beans: not actually beans, these are fermented carob pods. Slightly sweet, and slightly unpleasant smelling, these mellow when cooked to add intense flavour to Nigerian soups and stews as an alternative to the ubiquitous Maggi seasoning cubes.

Lulo: this tropical fruit is also known as *naranjilla* or 'little orange'. It is used to make drinks in Colombia and tastes like a citrus version of a kiwi fruit.

Mace: this is the thin red outer covering of the nutmeg. It is removed and dried before use. Left whole, it is known as a 'blade of mace'. It can also be used ground. It has a similar flavour to nutmeg but is warmer and spicier and usually used in savoury dishes.

Merguez: these are North African sausages made from lamb and flavoured with chilli and flavours such as cumin, fennel, coriander seed and paprika. They can be quite spicy.

Michelada: a popular Mexican drink made from beer and Clamato juice, it is further spiced with Worcestershire sauce and celery salt, and then served with a lime and salt-rimmed glass. It is similar to a Bloody Mary, but better for drinking in hot weather.

Moi moi: a Nigerian favourite, this steamed pudding is made from black-eyed peas. Usually savoury and containing hard boiled eggs, tomatoes and peppers, it can also be served sweet with apples.

Mulam: this is the term for a professional *suya* chef in northern Nigeria. Each has their own spice blend and style of cooking the meat.

Nori: an edible seaweed which the Japanese eat in sheet form, it is used to wrap sushi rice.

Nurishment: a Caribbean fortified milk drink sold in metal ring pull cans, it comes in flavours like chocolate and vanilla and is very thick, like a milkshake. It is drunk on its own or as part of Guinness Punch.

Obachan: the Japanese name for the woman who runs an *okonomiyaki* shop in Osaka.

Okra: also known as 'lady's fingers', *bhindi* in India, *okura* in Japan and *ochro* in Trinidad, these are star-shaped seed pods from the mallow family. Sometimes perceived as slimy, they are used to thicken soups and stews. Only use firm, non-sticky pods. This will prevent any sliminess.

Oleleh: this is a mix of beans, onions and seasonings from Sierra Leone. Sometimes mixed with fish and tomatoes, it is steamed inside banana leaves and sold across the country as easy-to-eat street food.

Otsumami: the Japanese term for small tapas-style dishes.

Palava: this is a dish worth making a fuss about. A traditional West African dish, it features a mixture of spinach or beet leaves, dried prawns, smoked fish and meat, and is thickened with *egusi* or melon seeds. It is thought to be the basis for *callaloo*, having been brought to the Caribbean by slaves.

Palm oil: one of the few saturated vegetable fats in nature, palm oil is derived from the fruit of the oil palm. It is identifiable by its reddish colour and semi-solid texture at room temperature. It is this style of palm oil that is used extensively in West African cooking for its colour and flavour rather than the heavily processed version used in processed foods.

Palm sugar: this is made from the sap of the palm date which is boiled and formed into hard round cakes. These are then grated or melted before use. Known as *jaggery* in India, it is often used to make sweets. In Thailand, it is used to give the sweetness in the traditional combination of sweet, sour, spicy, salty and bitter that makes Thai cuisine so popular.

Palm wine: an alcoholic beverage made by fermenting the sap of the palm date, using the natural sugars and yeasts present in the sap. It is drunk throughout West Africa and Asia and is known as *toddy* in India and Sri Lanka. Cloudy in colour, it has a sweet, slightly musky flavour and is around 5% alcohol. It can be distilled further to create a strong spirit known as *arak*.

Panko breadcrumbs: Japanese breadcrumbs made by passing an electrical current through bread dough instead of baking to make light crunchy crumbs without any crust.

Pigs' tails: quite simply, this is the tail of the pig. Usually sold salted or smoked, they are used throughout the Caribbean and American South to add flavour to dishes. They are particularly flavoursome when slow cooked with leafy greens and pulses.

Pimento peppers: often used to mean the small piquant heart-shaped pepper used to stuff olives or served pickled. It is also used to mean 'ripe red bell peppers' in Portuguese. Not to be confused with pimento berries or allspice, it is so named because Spanish explorers thought they were black pepper.

Piri-piri: the Mozambican word for the 'bird's eye chilli'. Mixed with garlic and lemon it also known as 'piri piri sauce' by the Portuguese who colonised Mozambique. It is famous on chicken but can also be used on seafood, fish and vegetables. Each version is unique.

Plantain: a member of the banana family, they are traditionally larger in size and lower in sugar than bananas. They come in two varieties – either unripe (or green), or ripe. Both must be cooked before eating. Unripe plantains are starchy and almost bread-like in texture with a bland flavour. Ripe plantains with their black and yellow skin are stickier and sweeter.

Porcini: also known as *Boletus* or 'ceps', these are a wild mushroom with a strong flavour and distinctive texture. Sometimes available fresh in southern or central European countries, they are more commonly available as dried mushrooms.

Red snapper: a type of fish from the warm waters of the Gulf of Mexico and commonly eaten in the Caribbean.

Roti: an unleavened flatbread not just eaten in the Indian subcontinent, but particularly associated with Trinidad and Tobago and Guyana where it is used to wrap round curried dishes as popular street food.

Saltfish: this is a generic name for any dried and salted white fish. Traditionally it was made from cod, which is highly prized but often overfished, making pollock and other white fish more popular. Both are used throughout the world but are especially popular in the Caribbean and Mediterranean. The fish is rehydrated before eating and doesn't taste salty.

Sake: a Japanese alcoholic drink made from rice fermented in a process similar to beer-making. It can be served both warm or chilled. One of the oldest kinds of alcohol in the world and so intrinsic to Japan that the word 'sake' often refers to all alcohol there.

Scallion: the Caribbean name for 'spring onion'.

Scotch bonnet peppers: rather delightfully named for their resemblance to the Scottish Tam o'Shanter hat, these squat little chilli peppers pack a real punch. Around ten times hotter than jalapeños, they are widely used in African and Caribbean cooking as they have a distinct fruity flavour as well as heat. They are often used whole in soups and stews to infuse flavour without the kick. They are not to be confused with habanero peppers.

Seasoning: in the Caribbean, 'seasoning' refers to the mix of bell peppers, spring onions, onions and scotch bonnet peppers that are sautéed as the base of many dishes.

Shichimi tōgarashi: Japanese 7 spice seasoning. It contains red chilli pepper, black sesame seeds, white sesame seeds, dried tangerine peel, dried seaweed (*nori*), ginger and *sanshō* (Japanese prickly pepper). It has more depth and flavour than simple chilli.

Shiitake mushrooms: these deeply flavoured mushrooms hail from Asia and are popular in Japanese cuisine. They are available fresh and dried.

Shoyu: a wheat-based soy sauce with a deep umami flavour. The gluten enhances the depth of the flavour.

Shrub: in cocktail terminology, a 'shrub syrup' is one containing sugar and an acid such as vinegar or lemon juice. Originally designed to preserve gluts of fruit before refrigeration, they are now primarily used to quench your thirst while stimulating your appetite so that sweetened drinks don't become sickly.

Spirulina: a dark green sea algae rich in nutritional qualities. Particularly useful in a vegetarian or vegan diet, it is high in vegetable proteins and B vitamins, especially B12. Easy to digest, it is mineral rich and believed to boost energy naturally. It comes powdered.

Stockfish: this is dried cod, usually from Norway. The fish is opened out and has the guts and head removed, keeping the shape of the fish. It is air dried, rather than salted, until it looks like a stick. It is rehydrated during cooking and, while it is popular throughout the world, it is commonly eaten in West Africa to flavour soups, stews and staple dishes like yam. See them outside Kumasi Market.

Tahini: ground sesame paste. Most commonly associated with hummus, it is a versatile ingredient. Look for a loose consistency like the **Al Nakhil** brand with its distinctive green lid.

Tamarind: this tree fruit is used throughout Africa, South East Asia and the Caribbean to add a sour, sharp and slightly sweet flavour to food. It usually comes as a block of pulp that must be soaked in hot water and then strained through a sieve to make a smooth purée. If you are in a rush, you can buy it ready-made but it's not as good. It is one of the key ingredients in Worcestershire sauce.

Taro: the most common name for the plant *Colocasia esculenta*, its roots and leaves are used throughout the world as a staple crop. The tubers are used to make flour in both sweet and savoury dishes. The leaves are sometimes called 'elephant ear plant' due to their shape. *Eddoes* are a smaller variety of **taro**. It is known as *cocoyam* or *dasheen* in West Africa and the Caribbean.

Teff: a hardy species of grass grown in the Horn of Africa and particularly prized in Ethiopia and Eritrea. High in calcium and protein, *teff* grains are milled into a gluten-free flour used to make *injera*.

Tilapia: a primarily fresh water fish commonly eaten in Africa.

Trebbiano: an Italian grape variety used to make white wine of the same name.

Triple sec: a colourless orange-flavoured liqueur based on brandy, it is used in margaritas, but you can use Cointreau instead.

Umami: the fifth taste along with sweet, salty, bitter and sour, it is intensely savoury and found in things like mushrooms and ripe tomatoes as well as meat.

Yam: a starchy tuber eaten throughout the world. Often confused with the sweet potato in North America, they come from a completely different plant family and are much more versatile. You name it, you can do it with a yam. Fry, mash, boil, bake, grill, barbecue, stew or grind into flour: the yam does them all. There are as many varieties of yam as there are ways to cook it. Yams can be served sweet or savoury and take other flavours well. They must always be served cooked as they are toxic when raw. They are known as *yamaimo* in Japan. In West Africa, yam flour is known as *fufu* or 'pounded yam' and mixed with water to make a thick dough to dip into soups and stews.

Xanthum gum: often used in gluten-free baking, it is used to thicken and stabilise food. It prevents gluten-free cakes from crumbling to nothing when baked as it gives a similar stretch and structure as gluten. A fermented corn sugar, it is safe for coeliacs and those with gluten intolerance to eat.

INDEX OF RECIPES

A

B

C

D

E

P

Q

R